W9-CAH-755

Performance Counts

Holding Learners Accountable in a Business Setting

By

Dr. Tony Alessandra, Frank Sarr, and Pamela Truax

Performance Counts. Copyright © 2001
by Frank Sarr, Training Implementation Services, Inc

Printed in the United States of America
First Printing: September 2001

ISBN: 0-9706992-0-4

Library of Congress Cataloging-in-Publication Data

All rights reserved. No part of this book may be reproduced in any
form, by any means, without prior written consent of the copyright
owner.

Cover and book design by Deena Quilty of Quilty Communications.
Edited by Doreen Friel.

For more information about *Performance Counts*, call 1-877-659-8847
or visit www.performancecounts.com.

FOREWORD

With the advent of Peter Senge's "Fifth Discipline" several years ago, corporate America and its global counterparts have embraced his concept of "Learning Organizations." Since that time, Human Resource Development (HRD) Professionals in progressive companies and agencies have continually proven their value in contributing to bottom-line results.

However, in far too many other organizations, the HRD function has been archaic in its thinking, and is often among the first casualties of downsizing companies. In this scenario, the HRD department is viewed as a "cost" rather than as "cost effective."

In this book, you will learn the difference—and, more importantly, learn how to utilize this approach in your own organization. The Accountability Performance System (APS) really can make that difference for you! Its three major components—i.e., its structure with Checkpoints and Final Assessment, its monitoring and thirdly, its accountability are proven tools to make any organization both measurable and, indeed, accountable.

Using the theater as a metaphor, you'll take a journey and see how the characters, i.e., director, players, reviewers, etc., all play important and integral roles in their real-world applications.

The APS has a proven track record. Its authors offer us a pragmatic and practical vehicle that addresses the critical issues and challenges facing us in this new millennium. Through a step-by-step process, you will have the tools you need to accelerate the continued growth of your top performers and identify those areas needing attention of others.

This important work will prove to be a priceless ally to help you ensure that all of your company's training and development efforts will possess that elusive transferability of training. Using actual case studies, you will see that APS has worked for numerous other companies. Now you hold in your hand, the power and the formula to make it work for you! *Do* it!

Edward E. Scannell, CMP, CSP; Past President, ASTD (American Society for Training and Development); Former Executive Chairman, IFTDO (International Federation of Training and Development Organizations)

Table of Contents

From My Perspective...
Tony Alessandra, Ph.D.

The longest journey on earth begins with a single step.
(Anonymous)

When people are given too much knowledge in too short a time period, panic sets in. Faced with new information, everyone needs to practice these new skills to see which areas fall into place and which don't.

New knowledge is much easier to absorb when a clear picture of a goal is presented. Dr. John Lee, a leading management expert, demonstrates this in his workshops by giving groups of participants a 70-piece puzzle to assemble. One group views a picture of the completed puzzle; the other groups put theirs together without knowing what the finished product will look like. Consistently, the group with the picture finishes first. Why? They already know their goal. They have the advantage of possessing a blueprint for success which they tackle one bite-sized piece at a time.

Can you remember when you first learned how to drive a car? Before you learned how, you were in the Phase One: "ignorance" stage. You did not know how to drive the car and you didn't even know why you didn't know how to drive it. When you first went out with an instructor to learn how to drive, you arrived at Phase Two: awareness. You still couldn't drive, but because of your new awareness of the automobile and its parts, you were consciously aware of why you couldn't. At this point, the "awareness" stage, you at least realized what you had to do to acquire the competency to drive. You may have felt overwhelmed by the tasks before you, too, but when these tasks were broken down one by one, they weren't so awesome after all. They became attainable. Step by step, familiarity replaced fear.

Similarly, in Phase Two, your people need to feel the exhilaration of small successes, interspersed with the inevitable mistakes that they must make while acquiring new concepts and skills...one step at a time. How can a manager move an employee from Phase One to Phase Two?

Books, cassettes, videotapes, films, weekly meetings, speeches, seminars, workshops and other learning aids can ease employees into awareness. Then, of course, the managers need to ensure that the newly found awareness (input) sticks.

With some additional practice and guidance, you were able to become competent in driving the car through recognition of what you had to do. However, you had to be *consciously aware* of what you were doing with all of the mechanical aspects of the car as well as with your body. You had to be consciously aware of turning on your blinker signals well before you executed a turn. You had to remember to monitor the traffic behind you in your rearview mirror. You kept both hands on the wheel and noted your car's position relative to the centerline road divider. You were consciously aware of all of these things as you competently drove. This third phase is the hardest stage—the one in which your people may want to give up. This is the "practice" stage. Your employees will make mistakes here. People tend to feel uncomfortable when they goof, but this is an integral part of Phase Three. Human beings experience stress when they implement new behaviors, especially when they perform imperfectly. As their manager, you must realize that they'll want to revert to old, more comfortable behaviors, even if those behaviors are less productive.

As their manager, you can play a crucial role by helping your team over the rough spots. It's all right for them to make mistakes. In fact, it's *necessary* to enable them to improve through practice, practice and more practice. Encourage them over these hurdles, and you and they will reap the harvest of your perseverance. Your job as manager is to assist them by again following up their new knowledge with concrete skill development. This can take various forms, according to the needs and wants of the group. Some examples for follow-through can be role playing; joint sales calls; exposure to repetitive messages, such as listening to instructional tapes en route to work; informal workshops to encourage skill development; or coaching and counseling the employee to assist in the growth process.

Returning to our car analogy, think of the last time that you drove. Were you consciously aware of all of the actions that we just mentioned above? *Of course not!* Most of us, after driving awhile, progress to a level of "habitual performance." This is the level where we can do something well and don't have to think about the individual steps. They come "naturally" because they've been so well practiced that they've shifted to automatic pilot. This final stage, then, Phase Four, is when practice results in assimilation and habit.

Our example holds true for your use of professional training through the first three relatively uncomfortable processes of ignorance, awareness, and practice in order to get to the blueprint for success—the highest level of "habitual performance." Only then can they use the training techniques naturally and effectively. If you can get your people to that level, you should see an increase in their productivity. However, you and your staff must pay a price to get to this level of competence: repetition and more repetition.

When you were learning to drive the car, you acquired your competency through practice. The same holds true for work skills. New skills will probably require a change of behavior from your team's present method of working. If this is the case, expect to see an initial decrease in productivity. This is a common occurrence in behavioral change. However, as they approach the automatic level of working through persistence and practice, their productivity will increase beyond its previous level and reach a new and higher plateau.

This four-phase model for success can help you and your people break out of the rut most of us dig for ourselves. By experiencing success and encouragement at each level, change can be exciting instead of intimidating. The bottom line is this: skills and attitudes will both improve by taking one step at a time with you, as manager and/or trainer, implementing support systems and skill development sessions along the way—and that is where the Accountability Performance System comes into play.

I work hard at perfecting a presentation that is motivational, educational, and contains the examples that enable the listeners to say, "Aha, I get it." In addition to "getting it," I want the listeners to go back to their jobs and apply what has just been presented to them. Why? Because what was presented works, it will accomplish everything that I said it will, and I have devoted a large part of my speaking career to fine-tuning what I am presenting so that it will be easy to understand and apply.

People actually leave the presentation motivated to apply what they have learned. Then, the realities of the remaining business sessions of the meeting and/or their work day set in. Only the extremely motivated attempt to take what they have learned to the next level—implementation.

It is at this point that my clients tell me that this was great material—exactly what their people needed. Then, the client asks how to follow up to make certain that they use what they were exposed to in my presentation. Based on the applause and the interaction with the audience, I know and am enthused about the fact that the participants were "into" my presentation. I might even conclude that they understand what I was presenting to them. But can they apply what they have learned? If I were to ask any one of them to *discuss*, *explain* or *demonstrate* what they learned from the presentation, how many of them really could? But this is exactly what a follow-up program has to address. I have books, videos, and cassettes that are used for follow-up. But what I didn't have was a *process*. A process that would enable my clients to take control and measure how well the participants are able to *discuss*, *explain* or *demonstrate* the critical concepts that they learned, not only from my presentation, but also from the activities they have to perform as part of a follow-up process. I want as many of them as possible to move from understanding the concepts to being able to apply them in their jobs, when interacting with their family, and in their daily lives.

The Accountability Performance System provides the process needed to empower employers to put into place the structure that is required to ensure that learning is going to take place. In the context of the Accountability Performance System, the learner **owns** the responsibility to learn, the "trainer" facilitates the learning, and the employer establishes the accountability for the learning. Each has to carry out their individual responsibilities if learning **by the learner** is to be maximized.

The Accountability Performance System added a needed dimension to instructional design by providing its users with the answer to the "how," not just the "what." The "how" works for all audiences and subject matter—which is its beauty. In other words, the process never changes. The implementers, once they understand the process, implement each new subject exactly as they implemented the last subject. The Accountability Performance System was developed because it was determined that if we wanted to make managers more effective in delivering their training responsibilities—which in their position descriptions represents 5%, 10%, or 15% of their overall responsibilities—we needed to give them a management process to make them more effective "trainers" rather than "train them to be trainers."

From my perspective, the Accountability Performance System works so well because it:

- Enables managers by giving them a process to carry out their training responsibilities more effectively. This is an approach that I had not seen before, immediately saw its merits, and recognized that it addressed the training and learning needs of my clients.

- Surrounds the concepts and principles I have worked so hard to develop and refine over the years with a "how" versus "what" implementation process. The APS will enhance their successful implementation and dramatically increase their value to my clients.

- Moves learning from an event to a process, which is exactly how learning should take place.

Introduction

Performance Counts is a book about improving your bottom line by implementing a successful, measurable learning process. This book is directed at decision makers with responsibility for business results. The second target audience is savvy corporate training directors, instructional designers, or Human Resource managers.

We promise to challenge your assumptions about the way training is structured and the decisions that are made about training budgets, interventions and promised outcomes.

If you are successfully conducting training programs that are accountable **and measurable**, congratulations. We do not mean you when we discuss training as "the sinkhole of organizations," where bagels, coffee, and smile sheets define the day and participants leave with an uneasy feeling that *good* or *bad* evaluations had no relationship to sustaining learning.

A training program should be structured with the end in mind: the actual successful performance of a person responsible for a business function.

Most training programs have this *intent*, but **implementation** falls far short of the intended result. Why? Because accountability is absent. This book sheds light on accountability in training, and provides a platform that builds accountability into the design of training programs.

Given a widespread discontent with training results, hip training talk currently focuses on technology as if *that were the answer.* Yes, on-line training can certainly help improve results. What is missing in those water cooler and boardroom discussions about training effectiveness is the underlying question, *How does learning take place?* Regardless of the modality—sit-down training or on-line training—the learner must take the time and make the mental space to integrate skills and/or information into her whole being, not as a good idea, but as a part of herself. Whatever the subject, proficiency occurs because the learner *makes* it happen. Period.

The Accountability Performance System described in this book creates a context where the learner is 80% responsible for his own learning. It taps into the psychology of what makes people accountable. Accountability flies in the face of a natural complacency that arises on the job. In contrast, new hires bring an eagerness and willingness to learn. Some call this eagerness the "ideal performance state." The Accountability Performance System both capitalizes on that ideal performance state of new employees and recaptures it for other employees.

The Final Assessment is the clincher that ensures sure-fire accountability. After the victorious learner has passed the Final Assessment, Frank Sarr of Training Implementation Services often asks the question, "Would you have done this work and performed this well without the Final Assessment?" The answer is always and inevitably, "No."

Skills and Knowledge Transfer = the "Measurable" Result

In this book, we focus on one context, sales, where profit and revenue growth are the desired end. Every company sells something, every company measures the effect of sales (i.e., financial success), and so every company executive can relate to the sales context. You can create a measurable outcome with the Accountability Performance System in customer service, administration/operations, quality assurance, and production—**wherever people are responsible for results and where measurement occurs.** The Accountability Performance System does not leave measurement to chance. It incorporates measurement into the design of the process as a Final Assessment. The Accountability Performance System can be applied to any training program currently on your shelves—as well as to those yet discovered or created.

Where Is Your Pain?

We asked field managers at a major financial services company what training issues they faced. They named the following nine:

1. No ongoing assessment to monitor the results of training.

2. No consistency in training from one group of trainees to another.

3. Inaccessibility of existing training resources.

4. Little if any coordination of materials to follow a logical flow of delivery.

5. Challenges in scheduling training; for example, one person needs training but not a whole group of people, or scheduling conflicts in general.

6. No/poor monitoring of the training that is taking place.

7. Difficulty in providing training to detached locations where there is no trainer.

8. Lack of retention in time-intensive training classes.

9. Dealing with and justifying the overall cost of training, given the poor or questionable results.

These managers were feeling the pain of not getting the results they desired. But they were unable to address this problem. Meanwhile, the training department continued to deliver a high volume of training programs, without providing a platform to successfully deliver these programs to their individual offices, and without addressing the pain expressed by their field managers.

Accountability Pays!

To alleviate the pain, the Accountability Performance System administers a heavy dose of accountability for managers and their trainees.

Frank recounts the following. One day, he was visiting an insurance company client. His contact, the vice president of sales, met him in the reception area. As they walked to the VP's office, Frank observed clusters of salespeople in conference rooms on either side, heads bent over notebooks. They could hear murmurs and Frank asked the obvious question:

"What are they doing?"

"They're preparing for the next Checkpoint," the VP responded, as he stuck his head into one conference room and teasingly said, "I hear the Chairman of the Board is going to be one of the assessors for the Final Assessment!"

To which they all responded, in unison, "NO!"

The Accountability Performance System, which Frank had introduced to this company, was directly responsible for the intensity with which these salespeople studied, and not at the times when they were expected to be working with prospects and clients. Knowing it is human nature to shoot the messenger, Frank made himself as invisible as possible. The VP, on the other hand, was laughing. Having been a participant himself, the VP understood what these learners were going through. Furthermore, he would administer the consequences for those who failed the Final Assessment. But he also knew the victory celebration that would follow for those who successfully completed the Assessment. Accountability has its penalties AND its rewards.

PRELUDE: THEATER AS A METAPHOR

A metaphor uses one idea in place of another through analogy to explain and clarify. Metaphors are useful teaching tools because they help the reader readily understand core principles and lessons.

Terminology of the Theater Metaphor

Most people are familiar with theater, but not everyone is conversant with designing successful training programs. Therefore, this book will describe the Accountability Performance System using theater as a metaphor, because it loosely parallels what occurs when a company uses the Accountability Performance System in lieu of, or in conjunction with, traditional training.

Author

The "author" is the corporation (client) that offers up reams of training resources—three-ring binders that have sat on the shelf gathering dust. Some of these binders contain good content that can be freshened and recapitulated/recapitalized to support the current strategic objectives of the company. The Internet, the company intranet, brochures, the company's strategic plan, or any other relevant sources of information might also be incorporated into a customized Accountability Performance System.

Playwright

The "playwright," until now, has been Training Implementation Services (TIS). Based on extensive client interviews, TIS first weaves company resources into an *Accelerated Learning Guide* that is the road map used by learners, managers, and top executives. Frank Sarr's learning technology, the Accountability Performance System, is the subject of *Performance Counts,* which also provides information about the production of the *Accelerated Learning Guide*.

Script

The script is outcome-based and created from your selected resources. The *Accelerated Learning Guide* breathes life into your existing resources. The learner can use it to prepare for his Final Assessment and become more effective in carrying out his learning responsibilities and perform the core competencies that are taught.

Producers

Producers are the businessmen of theater. They hire assistants and designers, provide administration, and are responsible for financial outcomes. In our metaphor, the "producers" are the CEO's, COO's, and VP's answerable for the ultimate business result. It is the producers for whom this book is written.

Producers don't have a preexisting agenda regarding HOW training is done. Their livelihood isn't affected by changing the paradigm of training, but they HAVE been affected by the ineffectiveness of many traditional approaches to training, on-line and off. If you are a producer, responsible for business results in your organization, and you have become jaded about training, read on!

Set

The set is the context—whether it is sales, production, administration, or customer service—within which the learning is delivered.

Rehearsals

Formal rehearsals are Checkpoint Meetings, as short as 15 minutes and as long as 60- to 90-minute gatherings with the manager to confirm learner progress, or send up a red flag regarding the individual's effort or learning issues. Casual meetings of learners prior to Checkpoint Meetings are helpful for learning lines. These informal sessions are self-generated by and with fellow actors. Producers, if you see that your people have many informal sessions, it is a good indication that they are performing well as a team.

The terms "rehearsal" and "Checkpoint Meetings" will be used interchangeably in this book.

Directors

Directors are responsible for everything artistic in theater. As you might have guessed, directors are those who train. In different organizations, trainers hold various titles. Often, when there is no training department, managers perform the trainer role, taking a proactive (but not time-consuming) role of checking on learners to ensure they are progressing toward the Final Assessment. These short meetings are called Checkpoint Meetings.

The terms "director" and "trainer" will be used interchangeably.

To be effective, the director must:

- Have a good understanding of the context (set)—the reality in which their training is being delivered.

- Determine how the "lines" should be delivered (knowledge of the company, the manner in which they must approach their job).

- Provide the "script" that the trainee must follow to prepare for the dress rehearsal. The "script" is the purpose of the *Accelerated Learning Guide*.

- Monitor—locally, regionally and/or nationally—how well the trainee is developing her lines and following her script to anticipate how she will perform in the dress rehearsal and, ultimately, on the job.

The role of director is one of:

- Clearly communicating the value of the *Accelerated Learning Guide* (script) to learners and management.

- Preparing the cast to consistently deliver outstanding dress rehearsal performances.

- Remaining committed to the success of each and every participant, as though it were her performance at the dress rehearsal.

She does this by:
1. Choosing resources that present the ideas that she feels must be learned and understood.

2. Taking a facilitator/coach role (listening, encouraging), rather than teacher/trainer (telling). She is a guide by your side, rather than a sage on the stage.

3. Conducting Checkpoint Meetings where learners are required to demonstrate their understanding by "performing their lines" until the director knows they understand.

4. Being tough in Checkpoint Meetings to reinforce the performance expectation of the Final Assessment.

5. Taking the necessary actions to deal with the non-performers.

Actors

Actors are the learners who traditionally sit, listen, participate, and often forget because they are not measurably responsible for their own learning. In the Accountability Performance System, they are 80% responsible for their own learning—not just to memorize, but to personalize, then naturalize, their lines until the character emerges. The character is someone who knows how to perform their competencies so naturally and thoroughly that the likelihood of on-the-job success is very great.

The only way the performer can prepare is to practice, practice, practice. This practice is not done in the classroom, but on the performer's own time, in anticipation of delivering his lines to the director at rehearsals.

In order to deliver the lines in a convincing manner, performers must go beyond memorization to personalize these lines and then speak them as if they were their own words, naturalizing with their own emotions. THIS is mastery. A concert pianist runs his fingers over the keyboard, repeating the notes time and time again until they become music. A professional actor reads his lines, then memorizes them and repeats them until he becomes the character in the play. The role becomes enlivened as the actor goes from memorization to assuming the character. The steps are to memorize, personalize, naturalize.

The structure of the Accountability Performance System is based on an understanding of the continuum of retention, which is not our invention, but rather the result of years of research into human behavior. People remember and apply 10% of what they read, 20% of what they hear, 40% of what they hear AND see, 70% of what they verbalize and 90% of what they do. Actors move through these five steps to prepare for their dress rehearsal.

In the theater, actors read their parts to each other for the first half of the rehearsal schedule. Also, blocking (learning the actors' positions on stage) takes place and characters become familiar with their respective roles. At home, they memorize their lines. In this early stage of the rehearsal schedule, they are hearing and seeing, which are retention steps toward being able to apply what they have learned. Mid-point in the rehearsal schedule, they go "off book," which means they give up their scripts and begin to "say" their lines, which are memorized, while moving around the stage to practice the combination of "say and do."

Likewise, the trainee must repeat the core words required in her job until they become her music, her character lines, as familiar as her own name. The terms "actor," "trainee," and "learner" will be used interchangeably.

Dress Rehearsal

The dress rehearsal is the Final Assessment, where the learner discusses, explains, and demonstrates his knowledge in front of an assessor. The more rank the assessor holds, the more accountable the learner will naturally be. This reflects human nature. Said another way, **the more performance anxiety is built into the Final Assessment experience, the better the results.**

The Final Assessment is the learner's last opportunity to mimic the real-world experience. A triumphant dress rehearsal is one in which the actors integrate the director's ideas and their own hard work and intense preparation into an extraordinary performance. **An extraordinary performance by ordinary people is the mission of the Accountability**

Performance System. The dress rehearsal marks the end of the training. The performance at the dress rehearsal simulates what you can expect from the learner when she interacts with a customer, fellow employee, or prospect on the job.

Upon completion of the dress rehearsal, sometimes the following questions are asked to get a better understanding of the total experience for the learner:

1. What was your reaction when you were told there would be a "dress rehearsal?"

    Typical answers: "We didn't like it." "We thought it would never happen." "We got upset and angry."

2. What impact did your expectation of the "dress rehearsal" have on your preparation?

    Typical answers: "When we knew they were serious, we got into it." "When it didn't go away, we started to panic." "It forced me to do what I would not have done otherwise."

3. What if I told you when you arrived for your dress rehearsal, that we were not going to have one, that it was a joke?

    Typical answers: "I would have been mad as hell." "I worked too hard to have you blow this off."

4. Tell me another way I could have gotten you to read the assigned material, view the videos, go to your intranet, complete the assignments necessary to prepare yourself for the Final Assessment and learn what you needed to know in order to do your job more successfully?

    Typical answer: "I can't think of any other way."

The terms "dress rehearsal" and "Final Assessment" will be used interchangeably.

Opening Night

Opening night is the real-world experience, where the trainee uses what he has learned. In the case of sales, opening night would be the first client meeting. The play becomes business for real.

Curtain Call

The curtain call signifies the result or the effect of the learning. In sales, the curtain call is the successful sale, signed and delivered. In consulting, it is a successful intervention. In lean manufacturing, it is more demonstrable efficiency on the line or, increasingly, in the office as lean thinking becomes more prevalent.

Reviews

Reviews appear in the newspapers after the opening night, reflecting a theater expert's perspective on the play. In sales, this might be a testimonial or, better yet, a qualified referral.

BROADWAY PLAY

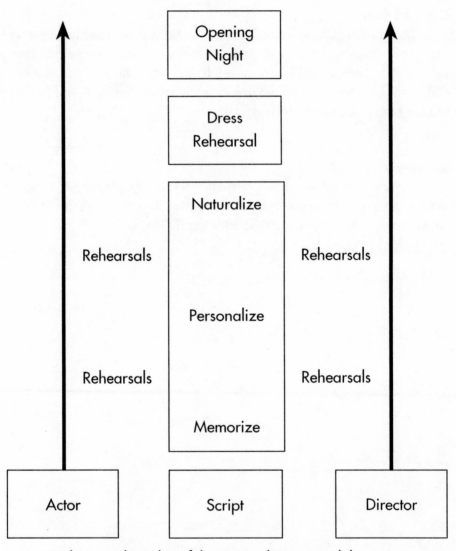

What are the roles of the actor, director and the script
to prepare for their opening night?

ACT ONE: PRE-PRODUCTION

Pre-production is important to identify the actors we want to move to a higher level of performance and consistency, and those who will be identified as poor performers. Early identification of poor performers is one bottom-line result promised by the Accountability Performance System.

Financial Results

Bottom line: *Performance Counts* shows you how to:
- Accelerate the growth of new and existing people.
- Accelerate the identification of people who need additional sup-. port to perform as expected or who are not going to perform as expected.
- Get your own valuable training resources used and identify critical learning resource gaps.
- Create accountability for learning results and performance.
- Improve the effectiveness of the "part-time trainers" who are implementing the training, while not requiring a lot of their time.

If you could do this, what would the financial implications be for your organization? The answer should be dramatic.

For example, in a sales context, you have two different sets of actors. New hires come in ready to learn. Existing salespeople, however, have habits; some good, some bad. The quality of these habits differentiates the top performers from the average performers and the poor performers.

Consider the Wall Street reaction to a publicly traded company when told that 35% of a 1000-person sales force—350 salespeople—might be terminated under a proposed approach to increase the productivity of the salespeople who had been with the company for three years. Frank Sarr had the experience of confronting 35% of a team of 1000 salespeople who were not meeting minimum standards, with the possibility of being terminated for non-performance, because of the expense of retaining these salespeople at this low level of production.

Sometimes management must face its own accountability in establishing and enforcing consequences for non-performance. This is not easy or without risk. How did these 350 people escape consequences previously so that the situation reached emergency proportions? Who permitted 35% of the sales force to become non-performing—that is, not even meeting *minimum* expectations? It sounds crazy, but this is a common occurrence.

A decision was made to put these 350 salespeople in a position to improve their performance and establish minimum production standards that, if not met, meant termination.

The company established a time period of 90 days in which individual development plans were built and in which these salespeople focused on activities necessary to achieve minimum production results. Individual plans spelled out training and support needed to help achieve these standards so long as the activity objectives were being met. Each individual plan was monitored.

A majority of these people did not leave because they increased their production to meet the minimum performance standards. That was not necessarily good news because it meant that even at minimum standards, these people were not very profitable to the company. The very existence of the standards, however, forced the salespeople to do what was necessary to retain their jobs until imposition of the next level of standards. Because of their lack of profitability, not much money was invested in these salespeople. But at least they were not costing the company money any longer.

> Top performers are the true or best actors in your play. These are the employees who will respond optimally to the challenge of this System. The Accountability Performance System will accelerate the performance of your top performers.

The time and money invested in this group of performers had to be kept to a minimum because there would not be a high return on the investment. The issue was not training. More than likely, they would not now miraculously overnight, or in the future, become top performers, regardless of the time and money invested. The best return on investment comes from your top performers.

Initiative, Preparation and Control Define a Top Performer

Based upon our experience, we know that top performers consist of 10% of the sales force. In the sales context, they share several important commonalities:

1. Top performers have many of the same characteristics of successful small business owners—both of whom operate as if they were straight commissioned salespeople.

2. They attain consistently high levels of activity from day one. Activity includes number of calls made, appointments made and kept, and number of proposals generated. This high level of activity persists from year to year. As they mature in their jobs, they fine-tune their skills and knowledge, move into better, more sophisticated markets, get direct referrals to decision makers, and build up their clientele without changing their level of activity that was high from day one.

3. Top performers are fundamentalists. They learn the basic skills, constantly refine these skills, and are always prepared to perform. That does not mean they are inauthentic. It means they are skilled and prepared, which gives them ample room to be authentic because the skills are "in their bones." Because of their skills, they are better equipped to listen, assess the needs of their prospects/clients and respond with solutions so that the prospects/clients will take action.

4. Top performers exhibit initiative, preparation, and control and represent about 10% of the productive sales force. When being trained, they use initiative to be in control, to succeed regardless of the environment, and regardless of the context, the program, or other people. Top performers do not wait to be shown what to do; they aggressively seek out best practices and processes. Their initiative enables them to "control the controllables." Preparation means drilling and rehearsing until they are prepared. They don't wait for prompting from the director.

Characteristics of the Middle 55%

Below that 10% is another 55% that produce above the minimum, but below the maximum. The minimum is defined as covering their expenses—office space, telephone costs, fringe benefits, secretarial support and so forth. The maximum would put them into the top performer group as defined above.

They have greater inconsistency in initiative, preparation and control; some start slowly, some start quickly and subside, some have spurts of activity.

1. They are more dependent on the "end of the year sale" to qualify for various honors.

2. They have wider swings in year-to-year production results as compared to top performers.

3. They are more diverse than the top performers regarding the range of development needs. Some need more sales skills training, some need to improve their technical knowledge, and others need to work on their business-owner mentality. They need to perform as if they were running their own business.

    These are the actors we want to move to a higher level of performance and consistency. The Accountability Performance System will quickly identify whether these people aspire to become top performers, average performers or poor performers. Those who are going to wind up as poor performers will be identified early in Checkpoint Meetings/rehearsals and may not even make it to the Final Assessment/dress rehearsal. Early identification of poor performers is one bottom-line result promised by the Accountability Performance System.

4. They require more supervision and management time to get prepared to present to their prospects and succeed in their careers.

Characteristics of the Bottom 35%

The bottom 35% complain a lot and produce below-minimum standards, meaning their results do not cover their expenses.

1. They generate marginal to poor activity from the beginning.

2. They tend to say the new product is uncompetitive, the new marketing program will fail and the economy is a disaster. They complain and ask for a better compensation program or better marketing support.

3. Very often, they are retained because managers fear losing their
    production, albeit unprofitable.

In comparison to the top 10%, who took the initiative, were prepared and in control, the bottom 35% say, "It's not my fault; it is someone or something else's fault."

What Each Group Needs From Management to Improve

Because of the differences just described, each group needs different training and development to take its performance to a higher level of
excellence.

The Top 10% Need to Be Handled
Like Successful Business Units

The Pygmalion Effect says that people rise to the level of expectations established for them. The higher the standards, the harder people
will work to meet them. Typically, top performers rise to the level they
have established for themselves. They don't wait for others to set their
performance standards.

Top producers need the kind of support that successful business
owners need to grow their businesses and live more balanced lives. They
need business planning, the creation of a plan to fill the gap between
where they are now and where they want to be. This is a unique developmental "gap" as identified by the salesperson and her manager, because
top performers are, by nature, always refining and improving. If the company does not address the developmental gap, it risks losing a top performer to another company that will fill the gap (or the top performer
may believe that the other company will do so) and he may jump ship.

The Middle 55% Need Customized Development Because of Their Diversity

Since this group is diverse in its response to the required tasks, one-
size training does not fit all. Using our sales context as an example, while
one salesperson may need more supervision, another may need more
product knowledge; another, better prospecting skills. The sales man-

ager must determine what these needs are and how to address them. The sales managers, to their surprise, may find that training is not the answer for some of the salespeople in the office.

The Bottom 35% Needs to be Awakened or Fired

The bottom 35% needs waking up. They must either recommit at a higher level—leaving excuses behind—and express willingness to be accountable for results, or be excused from their responsibilities.

The Accountability Performance System has been built for the top 10% and those of the 55% who want to be top performers. During the first 90 days, the Accountability Performance System treats everyone as if they were top performers and allows them to demonstrate what their own level of performance will be. This is why we say the Accountability Performance System will:

- Accelerate the growth of the top performers and would-be top performers.

- Accelerate the identification of the poor performers.

The Unmet Challenge of Training

What It Does

A good training program aims to change behavior by transferring skills and/or knowledge, which better supports the organizational goals and/or sales of a product or service. Despite the efforts of many sophisticated analysts, training programs have been perpetrated on organizations with very little accountability for results. The sad truth is that relatively few training programs result in substantial improvement in performance, and even fewer produce documented, measurable results.

Where It Falls Short

An article entitled "Thinking Outside the Evaluation Box" by Donna J. Abernathy in the February 1999 issue of *Training and Development* magazine recommends that you don't waste your time measuring the wrong thing just to check a box in the evaluation hierarchy.

What Our System Does

We agree that the effect of traditional training isn't what we want it to be; hence, the emphasis in recent years on accountability in training effectiveness. The Accountability Performance System delivers accountability and is the *platform* for holding learners accountable.

The Trainee Issue With Accountability

In training as in life, accountability is a core issue. Accountability makes people uncomfortable because they think they lack the resources to succeed and are afraid of failing. We don't WANT to see ourselves as successful because we would have to take responsibility for that success and for our results. The truth is that everyone is potentially powerful and with power comes accountability. Living anything short of powerful and accountable is cheating ourselves and everyone else who is affected by how we behave. One of the least understood paradoxes of life is that **accountability creates freedom and power,** which includes powerful results. Our perception of accountability must change. The Accountability Performance System forces participants to face their accountability and take responsibility for results.

The Trainer Issue With Accountability

Morris R. Shechtman, in his book *Working Without a Net*, says:

"As much as we may like to think that accountability exists in our workplace, we usually have nothing of the kind. Instead we've installed an ersatz version of this value. Organizations give the concept lip service, but they do not hold anyone truly accountable. They're reluctant because of the drive for comfort in our society; confrontation and conflict are often required to hold people accountable, and many managers would prefer to avoid making their subordinates and themselves uncomfortable."

Shechtman's accountability model delineates seven prerequisites for accountability that provide a useful backdrop for *Performance Counts*.

The first four prerequisites are inherent in the Accountability Performance System. The remaining three are tests of effective management.

Shechtman's Seven Prerequisites For Accountability

1. **Person to Person**
   Individuals are accountable to individuals, not to groups, committees or organizations. People are dealing with people.

   In training, this means the trainee must be put into a position where it is obvious to her that she is being held individually accountable for the learning outcome, even in a class or small group setting.

2. **Clarify**
   Clarify the areas in which one will be held accountable. Start with the job description to see if it accurately spells out the results for which the trainee will be held accountable in the business setting.

   Trainees are working toward competence in a specific job. Job requirements should be clearly spelled out.

3. **Set Expectations**
   Setting expectations in a specific and clearly differentiating manner will give trainees a clear target. A job description should include expected results, such as what, when, where, and how the job is to be performed. Clearly defining these expectations increases the likelihood that the trainee can be trained to meet and exceed them.

4. **Delineate Measurements**
   Delineate quantity and time frame as the measurements of accountability. In designing a training program, the measurements must be in place before the training begins. How will the expectations be measured? As an example, there are natural, logical points in a person's initial training to measure how well the trainee is progressing. The trainee should be held accountable for reach-

ing those points and for ***discussing, explaining or demonstrating*** what was requested.

Shechtman's first four prerequisites for accountability provide management with a structure to hold employees accountable. Some managers are unable or unwilling to risk relationships for the sake of results. Although the intent is to focus the feedback and consequences on the *behavior*, and not the *person*, some people lack the people skills to effectively keep the task and consequences separate from the personality. Managers can either mishandle or avoid confrontations and conflicts that arise from holding people accountable. When managers are accountable for results, Shechtman's prerequisites five, six, and seven are present.

5. **State Consequences**

   Managers state in detail the consequences for meeting or failing to meet established expectations. Both positive and negative consequences should be negotiated or agreed upon in advance of the training, so that the incentives for high performance after training exist before the training program.

6. **Enact Consequences**

   Enact consequences with immediacy, objectivity, and clarity.

7. **Top Management as Models**

   Top management are accountable themselves, modeling for others. If managers ask trainees to be accountable and they themselves are not, this engenders distrust and disharmony among employees.

Three Mind-sets That Affect Training Effectiveness

Three mind-sets impact any training program's successful implementation. The first of these three mind-sets drives the Accountability Performance System.

1. The Real Genius Is Not in Building "It," but in Getting "It" Used

There are many traps to choosing a focus when the need for training arises. One trap is your attitude about training. Three-ring binders sit in drawers and on credenzas across the corporate landscape; flotsam and jetsam of previous training investments give rise to resistance and resignation. The resulting attitude trap is *"training doesn't work."*

Another potential trap is technology. Virtual training is the future of many training programs, and rightfully so. But the focus too easily shifts to technology, with its costs and complexity, and away from the learner.

The set, or context, within which the Accountability Performance System functions, must be a primary consideration to the director. If the platform is implemented for the wrong reasons, it will sink like other training experiences, unless the director understands the mind-sets that influence successful implementation.

Quality training materials and technical resources and delivery systems are abundant already. Yet focus is too often placed on the training program, or the technology, and not on the learner and her long-term retention of the knowledge or skill. The Accountability Performance System can be applied to any training program currently on the shelves as well as to those yet discovered or created. The distinction between "content" versus "context" is useful because content is "WHAT" must be taught, and context is "HOW" the "WHAT" is taught. The Accountability Performance System brings the "HOW" to any "WHAT."

For example, you already have in your possession, or you can acquire, the materials and resources (albeit dormant, outdated or unused) that contain the core competencies your employees need. You can recapitalize these existing training programs utilizing the Accountability Performance System, with the focus being not on the resources, but on how to get them used.

In the initial stages of developing the Accountability Performance System, key questions are:

- What do we want the participants to discuss, explain and demonstrate as a result of the training intervention?

- How do we measure whether the participants can discuss, explain and demonstrate what will be used on the job, as a result of the educational experience?

- How do we continuously improve the process that enables people to discuss, explain and demonstrate their applicable lessons at a given stage of their development?

- How do we get the desired result for the trainee with the help of and/or in spite of the trainer?

When we enable the learner to discuss, explain and demonstrate what she has learned, chances are very good that she has integrated that learning into her being and will continue to demonstrate it on the job. Successful implementation depends on getting the materials to the learner so that she can discuss, explain and demonstrate what she has learned, *and* put in place the script and accountability needed for the learning to be accomplished.

2. This, Too, Shall Pass

Unsatisfactory results are the root cause of the feeling that *"this, too, shall pass."* If training has been a swinging door, a natural cynicism can arise and learners adopt a lackadaisical attitude, expecting that one training program will be replaced with another one soon, so why bother? For example, sometimes a new manager arrives and introduces his favorite training program, which may conflict with a previous one. At other times, a search for the perfect course means starting over. In this case, the "flavor of the month" conversation can be heard at the water cooler. When training programs are supposed to provide a quick fix, they rarely do. Each respective training program costs additional money because no one solution has been given a chance to either be effective, or to have its effect measured.

In this training climate, long-time employees are thinking and re-acting. Do any of these statements sound familiar?

- "Haven't we gone through this before?"

- "It sure sounds like the same thing to me, except they are using different terminology."

- "I put so much time into making the last program work. If they think I am going to change what I am doing now, they're crazy."

- "Why are they taking so much of my time when this is going to go away like the rest of these programs?"

Each successive training initiative becomes a greater credibility hurdle because learners have been trained mostly in "*this, too, shall pass.*"

3. You Can Produce the Greatest Dog Food in the World but if Dogs Don't Eat It, It Doesn't Matter

The third implementation issue has more to do with the playwright than the actor. The playwright is the designer of the original training program.

A well-packaged training program does not guarantee successful implementation. Sometimes designers do not pay attention to the desired outcome with the defined audience. One of three things can happen:

- The playwright spares no expense on packaging because the sale was made at a high level in the organization and a large budget enables fancy packaging.

- The program is designed based on ideal conditions instead of the reality of the context in which it will be applied.

- The program design is based on the playwright's interests and/or knowledge and not on the client's requirements.

You have to understand the implementation realities that exist in your organization. You have to see to it that what you are delivering gets used. To do this, you have to have an implementation strategy that gets the actor and director to pick up the script, look at it and know that they are going to become conspicuous by their using or not using the script.

A great training program built to the wrong outcomes is **not** a great training program. Training design *must* reflect the desired outcome and the needs of the learner, not the playwright. In the end, it is the performance that counts. A great training program creates productive employees who know and perform their jobs well.

The Other Side of Long-Term Retention: the Financial Implications

The financial implications of hiring the wrong people and not catching it can be substantial. The first 90 days are the most critical for the future success of any new hire. This is the point in development when the "right" hire is energized, focused, and anticipates intense training. Yet, even in sophisticated, traditional training programs that have elaborate monitoring and measuring processes, retention rates are a measly 9% to 13% of their salespeople after four years. Further examination revealed that these measurements of success were based on book knowledge and the ability to pass written and Computer-Based Training (CBT) tests, rather than on the ability to perform on the job.

If the Accountability Performance System were to ONLY reveal non-performing new hires, the cost savings would be astronomical.

Geoff Smart and Bradford D. Smart, Ph.D. conducted a study of the costs associated with mis-hires, and discovered that with an average base salary of $114,000, the average total cost associated with "typical" mis-hires was $2,709,000—nearly 24 times the person's base compensation.[i]

Even at $30,000, $50,000 or $60,000, the cost of a mis-hire is significant to the bottom line. According to the 1999 Emerging Workforce Study[ii] high turnover is not cheap. The survey pegs the cost of losing a typical worker at $50,000. So a 1,000-worker company making and retaining poor hires could lose millions of dollars.

Using conservative hypothetical numbers, if you hire 100 sales-people at $2,000 a month and retain them for 12 months, your cost is $2.4 million (see Chart 1, Line A). Statistics tell us that only 17% – 25% of the 100 remain after four years in the life insurance industry. So if you identify and eliminate 60 poor performers within 90 days of hire, the cost at $2,000 per month per person is $360,000 (Chart 1, Line B). The remaining 40 new hires are still with you after three months at a cost of $960,000 (Chart 1, Line C). The SAVINGS of having identified the poor performers within 90 days is $1,080,000 [$2,400,000 – 360,000 – 960,000 = $1,080,000]. You can do this analysis for your own company based on your knowledge of how many new hires remain with your company at the end of four years (or a time period of your choice). This analysis is based on one year at a very conservative per-salesperson cost. None of the overhead items attached with hiring are considered in this analysis.

Chart 1

A	100 new hires	X	$2,000/month	X	12 months	=	$2,400,000
B	60 new hires	X	$2,000/month	X	3 months	=	$360,000
C	40 new hires	X	$2,000/month	X	12 months	=	$960,000

Savings $1,080,000

We are not suggesting that these 60 people are not good people. We are suggesting that if you are going to lose 30%, 40%, or 50% of your sales force over, for example, a four-year period, why not identify those performers you are going to lose early in the development process and save yourself a lot of time and money?

If you are not witnessing extraordinary performances by new sales-people, you are not getting the best possible results.

The impact of not getting excellent results for the first 90 days from your people is that you:

- Are not maximizing the valuable time and money invested in the new hire.

- Squander the initial eagerness of the new hire to learn.

- Continue to invest new training dollars without focusing on the primary problems of ineffective treatment of that new hire in this critical stage of her career.

ACT TWO: BEHIND THE SCENES

To the naked eye, the Accountability Performance System is invisible. That is its strength. In a theater performance, there are many, many functions taking place that are not seen by the audience, yet they provide much of the effect that the audience receives.

Six Variables Illuminate the Need for the Accountability Performance System in Corporations

In the theater, someone is sitting in a booth illuminating the actors with colors and light on cue, providing the mood that appropriately supports the on-stage performance. Without it, the performance would be unappreciated and under-performed. The Accountability Performance System takes the unglamorous, off-stage role of supporting the play.

First, there are six variables that make the Accountability Performance System a solution to most corporate training shortcomings; and these warrant a brief description. Secondly, there are six factors of the Accountability Performance System that make it work.

The Six Variables

1. A preoccupied "trainer" is a manager who has many other responsibilities and may or may not have the skills and/or interest to develop her people through training. The end result: her effort and the effect are haphazard at best.

2. Training materials may or may not contribute to the success of a training event. Too often, well-thought-out binders or other potential learning resources are not used, not organized, and not appropriate, or out of context with the desired result. It looks like an overwhelming task to manage the materials, particularly to an overtaxed manager.

3. The learning environment is not well-managed, whether because of multiple training locations—each with its own approach to training—the strength or newness of the manager, the ability of the staff, the culture, or poorly communicated events.

4. The trainee can be in one of any number of states of readiness. For example, a new hire is generally in an "ideal performance state"[(iii)]—ready to take direction and seeking a place to channel energy. At the same time, he needs a sense of control, and is

willing and eager to be trained. Often this willing, eager recruit is left to wait for the next formal training session, while his psychic energy deflates.

5. Position stability. Restructuring, merging and downsizing create instability in the trainer's position. If a senior manager feels a sense of ownership of a particular training program and moves on, her enthusiasm and preparation are lost to her replacement. The newcomer, who wants that sense of ownership for personal or political reasons, reinvents the training, and trainers are now required to switch gears to meet the directives of their new senior manager.

6. Technology has made training more convenient for companies, but most learning is not "high-tech, high-touch." Too often there is no demonstration that the learning has taken place, no feedback mechanism, and no opportunity to support the learner through setbacks, confusion, lack of motivation, or any number of less-than-ideal mind-sets. And, just as importantly, the need to discuss, explain and demonstrate is not used as the mechanism to promote learning.

Given this as the traditional training environment, six factors make the Accountability Performance System a perfect solution where real learning must take place.

Six Variables of the Accountability Performance System

1	2	3	4	5	6
Learning Mission	Learner-Driven	Clear Expectations	Road Map (Accelerated Learning Guide)	Checkpoints to Discuss, Explain, and Demonstrate	Accountability

1	2	3	4	5	6
Learning Mission	Learner-Driven	Clear Expectations	Road Map (Accelerated Learning Guide)	Checkpoints to Discuss, Explain, and Demonstrate	Accountability

In many instances, learning is delivered through part-time directors—managers or supervisors whose other responsibilities get in the way of their being able to provide optimal training time and support.

Therefore, our mission is to put an *Accelerated Learning Guide* into their hands that, if followed, will produce extraordinary performances, regardless of the discrepancies from one director to another. It must be fail-safe. Inherent in the structure of Accountability Performance System is its ability to help managers:

- Accelerate the growth of new and existing people.

- Accelerate the identification of people who need additional support to perform as expected and/or who are not going to perform as expected.

- Get their own valuable training resources used and identify critical learning resource gaps.

- Create accountability for learning results and performance.

- Improve the effectiveness of the "part-time" trainers who are implementing the training (while not requiring a lot of their time).

The basic principles that are integrated into the Accountability Performance System's mission are:

- Successful people do things that failures don't like to do. In sales, this might mean calling on people who do not want to see them and talking to them about something they don't want to talk about.

- Set high expectations knowing that people will rise to the level of those expectations. *(The Pygmalion Effect)*

- Memorize, personalize, naturalize. Another way of saying this is practice, practice, practice. We will not sympathize with the trainees when they complain, but will hold our ground to keep them doing what they may not want to do, in honor of our commitment to excellence.

- If the wrong person is in the position, it may not matter what we do. The result will be the same. If we have the wrong person in the position, it will be acknowledged and we will administer the appropriate consequences to shorten the period of pain for all parties concerned.

- Tough love. Because accountability is so much a part of this process, there will be tension and the trainee may exhibit some stress about what is being requested. We must believe that the end result is worth the trainee's effort. Instead of sympathizing with the trainee, we will hold our ground, which keeps the trainee doing what he or she may not want to do.

- Don't assume. Just because we told or showed the trainees something, don't assume they know or can do it. We will check and double-check to make certain that trainees are competent in the areas in which we want them to be competent.

- Empowerment. We will give the appropriate tools to the right trainees and empower them to get something done, and we know the top performers will get it done.

1	2	3	4	5	6
Learning Mission	Learner-Driven	Clear Expectations	Road Map (Accelerated Learning Guide)	Checkpoints to Discuss, Explain, and Demonstrate	Accountability

There is a dramatic difference between self-study and that which is learner-driven. A learner-driven process focuses on what the trainee needs to discuss, explain and demonstrate if the skill or knowledge transfer is to occur. The distinction is made during rehearsals and the Final Assessment.

The key to success is self-motivated actors who will work independently to prepare for their performances. Setting expectations creates a sense of urgency. In addition, providing an appropriate level of tension contributes to learning. Rehearsals and the Final Assessment accomplish this. Participants who consciously create their own mission help themselves stay the course during the difficult aspects of training. Some possible learning missions might include:

- I will do *more than is necessary* to form the habits of a successful salesperson, which means I will get very good at forming habits that failures don't have.

- I will memorize, personalize and naturalize. In other words, I will practice, practice, practice.

- I will be true to my word and honor my commitments, even when I don't want to.

Gail Sheehy, in her book *Passages*, theorizes that we all go through predictable stages. She feels that if we understand the predictable dynamics of a given stage, we are better able to address those issues. The Accountability Performance System has identified the stages that a top performer goes through and about how long it takes for each to occur. It is structured to respond to each.

For example, the *ideal performance state* is present in a new hire when he joins the company. The right candidate automatically fuels the learning process and invigorates the trainer.

The delivery and focus of the training program should be appropriate to what the trainee needs, such as tight structure or daily feedback. **The receptiveness of trainees to being trained has a tremendous impact on the results, so the trainer will want to take responsibility for setting this up correctly: new hire versus existing employee, top performer versus marginal performer.**

1	2	3	4	5	6
Learning Mission	Learner-Driven	Clear Expectations	Road Map (Accelerated Learning Guide)	Checkpoints to Discuss, Explain, and Demonstrate	Accountability

Clear Expectations: Begin with the end in mind. Stephen R. Covey, in his book *Seven Habits of Highly Effective People*, points out that to operate in a highly effective manner, *you must first visualize what you are striving for and why*. One mistake people make in attempting to change how they conduct their lives is *focusing on tasks and forgetting about defining the end result*.

Our end result is to have trainees be able to *discuss, explain, or demonstrate* what they know or what they can do. Once those expectations are established, they can be put into a Final Assessment format. The Final Assessment is given at the end of the course, and all course material builds toward being able to perform at the Final Assessment.

A look at one section of a Final Assessment demonstrates how expectations can help motivate learners to prepare. There are no secrets; the questions that will be asked at the Final Assessment are included in the *Accelerated Learning Guide* given to the learner on the very first day she is introduced to the system; and all study is in preparation for being able to discuss, explain, and demonstrate proficiency.

The one-on-one Final Assessment is scored, utilizing a pre-established passing grade, and each section is weighted. Preparation (x) Weight = Score for each section. In the Appendix, on page **89**, you will find an example of a Final Assessment.

When we train directors to implement the Accountability Performance System, we have them experience the Final Assessment as if they were trainees. One reason is to give them a first-hand feeling for how the process works, and second, to enable them to empathize, rather than sympathize, with their trainees.

At the Final Assessment, the trainer is typically not the assessor because two people are being assessed—the trainee AND the trainer. The assessor is given the following instructions:

The role of the assessor is 90% listening, 10% asking the next question, then assessing the level of preparation/clarity of communication on a scale from 4 – 0. If the student comes prepared, the assessor will give high marks.

The trainee is expected to:

1. Show up

2. Show up on time

3. Show up on time, prepared

The dress rehearsal will test if the actor:

• Is prepared

• Took initiative to prepare

• Took control of what was required to come prepared

The student should come prepared to communicate what she knows. Her role will be 90% talking, then listening for the next question. She should communicate in a prepared and clear manner.

This may sound simple, but multi-million-dollar jobs require this basic level of clarity. Carmen Policy, owner of the Cleveland Browns, said about the person he hired as head coach, "I was shocked, actually. He just did his homework. I think that *preparation* for any important event is critical and certainly there is no greater attribute a coach (or fill in the blank with any other occupation) can have than to be well prepared."

Since the actor has the Final Assessment in her hands from the beginning of the process, she knows exactly what she will be asked to discuss, explain and demonstrate at the dress rehearsal. What would your reaction be if the actor showed up unprepared? Why would the actor come unprepared? How many of these reasons were non-training issues? The director is also being assessed through the performance of his actor. Why? Because if the actor performed poorly, the director should have never let the actor go on stage. If he did, then we know that the director did not play a role in the actor's preparation.

1	2	3	4	5	6
Learning Mission	Learner-Driven	Clear Expectations	Road Map (Accelerated Learning Guide)	Checkpoints to Discuss, Explain, and Demonstrate	Accountability

The script is a road map called the *Accelerated Learning Guide*. It contains all the lines that the actors must memorize, personalize and naturalize for their final rehearsal. (This script is not to be confused with a "sales script," which is a more specific and different document from the road map.)

This road map empowers the trainee:

1. To control the specific stages of his development.

2. To direct him to the resources he needs and pinpoint the information he must obtain from these resources based on his stage of development and need to know.

3. To measure his initiative, preparation, and willingness to take control of his learning.

4. To get to where he needs to be, *regardless of the teaching capability of the trainer.*

The *Accelerated Learning Guide* integrates all the resources into one user-friendly, manageable resource for both the trainer and the trainee. It can be used as a preparation tool for a traditional training session, as an entrance test to attend a training session, or with multiple trainers. Trainees who are monitored remotely by telephone, videoconference, or the Internet can also use it.

Additionally the *Accelerated Learning Guide* establishes a focal point for measuring the results. The trainer uses it to assure that the learner is on track to perform successfully at the Final Assessment. Management uses the same road map to monitor the efforts of both the trainee and the trainer.

The impact is different in different situations. For example, one of our clients had people whose careers, after 10 – 20 years, were stuck in a rut. Putting them through the Final Assessment made a difference. For example, one representative had been in the small business market her whole career. She

> Because everyone is working from the same road map, *no one can hide*—the learner, trainer, and management all have a measuring stick to determine the amount of effort being expended toward the Final Assessment.

didn't think she had the talent to expand into a more challenging position. The Assessment was the same for all the divisions. By providing an overview of all the different sales jobs, many people saw opportunities they hadn't previously entertained. After getting through the Assessment, she had learned enough about the large business market to see that it wasn't impossible to learn the specifics of this market. She wanted to get to the next level as a result. She was promoted to a large group based on her performance in the Assessment, which, by the way, was a surprise to management, who had an image of her that would have not given her the opportunity she sought without her preparation for and performance on the Final Assessment. She reports she has never been happier. She is making more money, has completely stepped out of her comfort zone, and continues her spiral upward.

In the Appendix, on page **95**, you will find an example of an *Accelerated Learning Guide* Introduction.

1	2	3	4	5	6
Learning Mission	Learner-Driven	Clear Expectations	Road Map (Accelerated Learning Guide)	Checkpoints to Discuss, Explain, and Demonstrate	Accountability

Rehearsals require trainees to continually prepare for their Final Assessment by having them discuss, explain, and demonstrate what they know. The first step is **memorizing. Personalizing** means internalizing so that you truly understand. Putting what you have read or seen into your own words, repeating the information over and over again so that it gets "into your bones" is **naturalizing.**

Memorizing, personalizing, and naturalizing make up 90% of rehearsal time. Some of the rehearsal time is spent alone, using resources and practicing. Some of it is spent with the director in Checkpoint Meetings. Some of it is spent with other learners in self-generated group practice sessions. These meetings are mini role-plays where the learner demonstrates progress and gets feedback. The actor's objective in this role-play meeting is to convince the director that he is prepared. The learner is performing, communicating, practicing and applying what he has learned. The director is observing, listening and data-gathering.

If the learner comes prepared to the Checkpoint Meeting, he performs in the manner shown below:

Indicators of Preparation				
Use of the Pause	Answers	Participation	Eye Contact	Spontaneity
Instead of "um.," "you know," "aah, ok?", the presenter uses silence to prepare to answer.	Presents concise, thought-out answers with a minimum of rambling or unnecessary elaboration or clarification.	Is ready when called upon to answer the question and is proactive in sharing constructive thoughts with the other participants.	Maintains eye contact and looks at you when giving the answer.	Responds to additional clarifying questions you may ask.

Evaluation of Performance		
High (H)	**Average (A)**	**Poor (P)**
Meets and exceeds the specific indicators of preparation.	In these specific areas of preparation she has not distinguished herself from the other participants.	Not prepared in these specific areas.

Checkpoint Meetings generate *observations*, *diagnosis*, and *next steps* for the actor. One objective of the *Accelerated Learning Guide* is to keep preparation work at a minimum for the director, so if corrective action isn't necessary, verbal acknowledgment will be sufficient feedback for the learner.

If there are performance shortcomings, the participant receives observations related to *knowledge and skills* for which they are studying; *attitude*, meaning he approaches assignments with a good or a poor attitude; and *habit*, meaning the pattern of behavior that emerges as the director observes this person. In the *Accelerated Learning Guide*, the *Diagnosis* section simplifies these observations into yes or no questions and answers.

Next steps are the activities and objectives required before the next Checkpoint Meeting, based on the director's observations. In the Appendix, on page **111**, you will find an example of the Checkpoint Meeting Performance Evaluation Form.

The learner gets instructional or introductory information in the *Accelerated Learning Guide*, but is then asked to study additional specific resources to prepare for the formal rehearsal. For instance, the *Accelerated Learning Guide* may send him to a 300-page resource, such as a corporate document, where only 20 pages apply. The Checkpoint Meeting occurs with no formalities. The manager just begins asking the questions that the learner was given in the *Accelerated Learning Guide* for that specific Checkpoint, where she was sent to the appropriate resources. The assumption going into the Checkpoint Meeting is that she is prepared. For instance, for a health maintenance organization, the first question for that Checkpoint might be, "Define HMO." Once someone answers the question, the trainer may then ask, "Jim, what's your definition?" "Mike, what are the characteristics of an HMO?"

The learner's objective is to convince the director that she came prepared.

This is an important distinction of the Accountability Performance System. At every Checkpoint Meeting, trainees know they are going to perform. Think about yourself. When you know you are going to perform, your stress level goes up. Your effort to prepare increases. You know you will not be able to hide. What the trainee prepares for demonstration, the trainee retains.

This has a positive effect on the learner, but it also has a positive effect on the director who, as we have seen, is often the manager with other responsibilities. The role of the director is a passive but important one of:

- Assessing whether the learner takes the initiative to get prepared.

- Listening to categorize the student's level of knowledge and ability to communicate that knowledge.

- Reflecting on whether this performance would impress a prospect, customer or client.

- Diagnosing the performance and the performer. Is this the right person to play this role?

How long should a Checkpoint Meeting take? If the trainee comes unprepared, then the Checkpoint Meeting is over immediately and the personnel discussion begins because the issue is one of hiring or personnel, not training. In this example, the Checkpoint Meeting itself took minutes; the performance discussion may have taken hours.

With a group of well-prepared trainees, the director controls the duration of a Checkpoint Meeting. After the actors perform, the director may enhance their knowledge and improve their chances for a successful Final Assessment. Checkpoints are ideally conducted with three to five learners, whereas the Final Assessment is one on one. You want Checkpoint Meetings to be structured so that top performers influence the preparation of the other participants through peer pressure. Additionally, a group might begin working together to prepare for the rehearsal; thinking as a team and self-regulating so that each member keeps up. They all want each other to succeed.

When the director is not certain how prepared participants are for a meeting, he keeps them performing by having them answer the assigned questions for the Checkpoint until he is certain they had prepared for the Checkpoint Meeting and are on track to pass the upcoming Final Assessment.

In the Appendix, on page **113**, you will find an example of a Checkpoint which the learner uses to prepare for a Checkpoint Meeting and the trainer uses to conduct the Checkpoint Meeting.

1	2	3	4	5	6
Learning Mission	Learner-Driven	Clear Expectations	Road Map (Accelerated Learning Guide)	Checkpoints to Discuss, Explain, and Demonstrate	Accountability

The dress rehearsal drives the performers to practice until they perform their scripts in a personalized and naturalized manner. In anticipation of the scheduled dress rehearsal, the actors and their directors also work on the nuances that will distinguish their performances from other performances of the same play.

Without accountability, training is not as effective as it should be and can be. Without holding the trainee accountable, the trainer can burn out because she, rather than the trainee, brings the energy to the training experience. The greater a student's acceptance of accountability, the more successful the student will be.

In preparation for the Final Assessment, the trainees are accountable for:

- Completing all assignments, orally answering all the assignment questions, and discussing the completed activities outlined in their *Accelerated Learning Guide.*

- Taking independent action when they feel they need additional resources or cannot locate materials assigned in the *Accelerated Learning Guide.*

- Asking for help when they need it.

- Coming prepared to answer the questions, demonstrate their skills or show that they completed their activities successfully.

- Being prepared to deliver an extraordinary performance at the dress rehearsal.

The trainer is accountable for:

- Setting the direction of the entire training process with the support of the *Accelerated Learning Guide.*

- Clearly communicating the training goals and methods, including the existence of the dress rehearsal by walking the trainee through the *Accelerated Learning Guide.*

- Demonstrating how to use the *Accelerated Learning Guide.*

- Making sure students understand their responsibilities from day one and reinforcing the message clearly and often.

- Knowing what trainees should accomplish at each Checkpoint Meeting/rehearsal, monitoring their activities and intervening if necessary to help them prepare for their Checkpoint Meetings. *(Note: the trainee who gets this attention must demonstrate that she is working hard to prepare for the rehearsals.)*

The combined existence of the *Accelerated Learning Guide* and the dress rehearsal allows all levels of management to monitor the trainee's development. This approach creates performance standards for rehearsals and the Final Assessment.

Our client decided to make successful completion of the *Accelerated Learning Guide* and subsequent Final Assessment the price of admittance to a new employee weeklong orientation meeting in the home office. The Final Assessment lasted 45 minutes, with the assessors asking a series of one-on-one questions.

According to the client, "At the Final Assessment, we had people who cried because they knew they were not prepared. The rule is, if you fail, we send you back and the manager pays for it; corporate won't pay. There were two times when that happened, and it was really sad, yet they had control and they chose not to take it seriously. Did we ever send anyone back? I think we did one time. Talk about low self-esteem at that point, because everybody else can attend the orientation and one person cannot. There was a lot of frustration, anxiety, sadness, anger, but we stood by the method and managers knew at that point we have to take it seriously. That person was terminated and the manager knew it better not happen again, which is a good thing and which proves the method works.

- The owner of the accountability is senior management.

- The owner of the Accountability Performance System is whoever top management delegates the responsibility of keeping the System operational.

"On the other end of the spectrum, each time they held an orientation, there was at least one person who knew the material inside and out; you could have asked anything and they were so confident and so good and so excited that it set the stage for a successful orientation. They were so proud of themselves. Whoever received the highest score received recognition from top management on the last day of the orientation.

"As the company hired new people, the first participants talked up the Final Assessment, saying to the new hires, 'You guys better be ready to perform.'

Throughout the week of orientation, people made comments like, 'You have no idea how afraid or how skeptical I was, going through this. But it was the best training I ever had!' Why? *Because they worked harder than they ever worked before and saw the return on the learning investment they made.*"

No One Can Hide!

The *Accountability Performance System* makes it possible to hold accountable all parties involved in the process. Let's go back to Shechtman's seven prerequisites of accountability and see how the system works within that model.

Accountability-Generating Tools		
Owner of the System	1. Accountability is to individuals, not to groups, committees or organizations. **Accelerated Learning Guide, Checkpoints** 2. Clarify the areas in which one will be held accountable. **Key Competency Areas of the Final Assessment** 3. Expectations must be stated in a specific and clearly differentiating manner. **Discuss, explain, demonstrate at the Final Assessment** 4. Measurement of expectations must delineate quantity and time frame. **Checkpoints, Final Assessment**	Owner of the Accountability
Management's Responsibility	5. Consequences for meeting or failing to meet established expectations must be stated in detail. 6. Consequences must be enacted with immediacy, objectivity and clarity. 7. Accountability must be modeled by top management.	

- The owner of the accountability is senior management.

- The owner of the system is whomever top management delegates the responsibility of keeping the Accountability Performance System operational.

ACT THREE: THE SCRIPT

In order to have a successful play, there has to be a well-written script that reflects what the actors should perform at the dress rehearsal and on opening night.

Curriculum Development Process

There are seven steps to creating the *Accelerated Learning Guide*. These steps include the Checkpoints and Final Assessment. The seven steps are:

1. ***Fact-finding.*** We ask questions inside the organization that lead us to the Final Assessment. We do not want to reinvent the wheel, developing materials that have already been produced. What starts out as a trickle of resources turns into an avalanche, especially when we use the company intranet as a resource. Fact-finding is sleuth work, a series of interviews and conversations within the organization, providing the fabric for weaving the tapestry called the *Accelerated Learning Guide*. For example:

   • We benchmark the training program against the best performers in the organization.

   • We interview management to confirm the need and to identify the unique company qualities that must be incorporated into the structure so that the Final Assessment accurately reflects management's strategic goals and objectives.

   • We ask questions pertinent to those strategic objectives, anything from mission and philosophy to expectations and business processes.

   • With subject matter experts, we identify the resources that will support the Checkpoint Meeting content.

   • We identify who needs to have buy-on so that these people support the program and we get them involved in the development and implementation process.

2. ***Designing the* Accelerated Learning Guide.** Even within the fact-finding phase, the major emphasis areas for the script begin to emerge through redundancy. This redundancy helps us define the Checkpoint titles for this particular group of actors.

In the design phase, we organize the content to reflect the culture, the processes, how the company wants its actors to project themselves to their customers, and what it will take for the company to say *"Yes, that's us!"* because they see their organization reflected back at them from the pages of the *Accelerated Learning Guide.*

- Once the knowledge/skills areas have been identified, we create a list of the competencies required to fulfill the learning objectives.

- We identify the questions that will make up the Final Assessment.

- We then begin to formulate the assignments and resources that are pertinent to gaining the competencies that will be discussed, explained and demonstrated at the dress rehearsal.

3. ***Building the Final Assessment.*** To be certain we are on the right track, we build the Final Assessment next because the Final Assessment determines the resources we will use. Final Assessment in hand, we go back to the company to confirm what the trainees will be expected to discuss, explain or demonstrate in each of the areas. We proffer a description of the proposed dress rehearsal and refine it according to the company's preferred emphasis.

4. ***Integrating Resources.*** This is the what, where, and when step that ensures that every competency has a resource to support its development.

- We identify markers within each resource to be used to support each competency and to develop the application questions that will test the trainee's ability in that area. Resources might include manuals, Internet, intranet, audios, videos, scripts, CBT courses, worksheets/forms, etc. These are the resources that the actors should be using in their job functions every day. So one objective of the process is to teach them to use existing resources as well as to successfully perform at the Final Assessment.

- Once the client approves the Final Assessment, Checkpoints, and resources, we mold the *Accelerated Learning Guide* into the format that is most user-friendly for them.

5. ***Developing Original Content.*** Based on activities up to this point and input from the client, we write the sections to convey information so skills transfer can occur. The content in each Checkpoint is intended to introduce the resources and subject matter in general, so the *Accelerated Learning Guide* can outlive the content in the resources, thereby providing ongoing value once adopted. The more specific the content, the sooner the *Guide* becomes outdated.

- The *Accelerated Learning Guide* singles out the resources that will supply the specifics. Because the customized content for the *Guide* is generic and conceptual, the resources are the only changeable elements in the *Guide*.

- This is a relief to the directors, who only have to learn one way to train. Resources come and go, get updated, become obsolete.

- Yet the inherent updating process keeps directors current about company changes indirectly, through new employees who are asked to deliver the new script.

6. ***Packaging.*** The final step is the packaging of the script. A three-ring binder is the most practical format, where tabs mark the four sections: Introduction, Checkpoints, Final Assessment and Appendix. For further user-friendliness, each Checkpoint has its own tab where the assignments, application questions, and activities related to that Checkpoint are organized.

7. ***Implementing.*** Once the *Accelerated Learning Guide* is complete, we have a platform to address implementation questions, such as "Should we send our directors through the process first?"

The answer is "Yes!" "How should we roll this out to our actors?" "When should we schedule the dress rehearsals?" "How do we make certain that we keep the script up to date?"

Over time, you must update the resources for timeliness and relevance based on feedback from the salespeople.

The length of the process depends on individual circumstances. For instance, completing an Accountability Performance System from zero knowledge of content to a ready-to-implement *Accelerated Learning Guide* takes three to five months if you are totally focused on the process outlined above.

On the other hand, if a base of information exists and you are simply personalizing the sequence, then the investment of time is considerably less.

If you were to make a snapshot of designing the *Accelerated Learning Guide*, it would look like this:

BUILDING THE SCRIPT

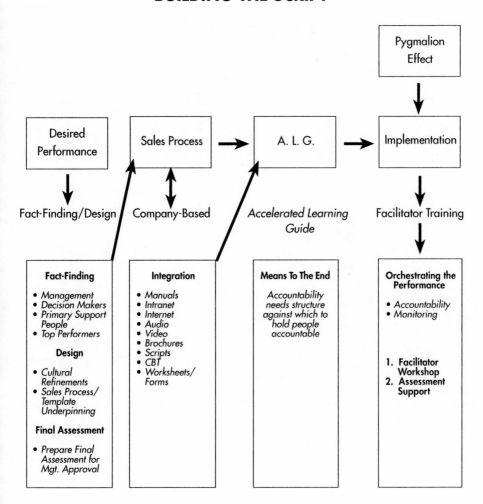

ACT FOUR: THE VENUE OF TECHNOLOGY

The theater venue itself can add or detract value from the experience of the audience. Today, the theater of choice is often interactive, distance learning, but learning comes from many sources, traditional and non-traditional.

High-Tech, High-Touch

High-Tech, High-Touch is a phrase popularized when ATM machines replaced tellers in many banks. It meant that for every technological innovation you create for customers, you should also be providing a personal touch.

There is no question that technology has made training more convenient. Instead of bringing employees to training, companies can reduce their training costs by bringing training to employees.

Today's training technology typically includes the Internet, teleconferences, videoconferences, virtual classes or some combination of these. As an aid to learning, these tools can disseminate information and provide feedback. What the Accountability Performance System can do with technology is increase the efficiency of learning. Nothing is lost from the inherent validity of the Accountability Performance System when applying it through technology.

For instance, the *Accelerated Learning Guide* can reside on an intranet. Checkpoints can be scheduled by phone, and the Final Assessment can be administered by videoconference (best) or telephone. Appropriate resources can be disseminated in any electronic form, including CD-ROMs or on-line training programs.

Building an Accountability Performance System for technology applications follows a logical process, many of whose steps are the same as a paper-based system. What changes is that once the resources are identified, the *Accelerated Learning Guide* is created in multi-media format, tested, and an activity tracking mechanism is applied. The Checkpoints and Final Assessment can be scheduled on-line, but they cannot be alleviated without losing the value of the Accountability Performance System. These are the high-touch aspects of the Accountability Performance System that provide accountability for the learner and differentiate this on-line training program from others.

Questions come up like, "We hire 1000 salespeople a year all over the country; how can we administer 1000 dress rehearsals?" One answer is videoconferencing, where the assessor and the learner can look each other in the eye for a very effective Assessment. Another answer is that if the Accountability Performance System is working, you will not *need* *1000* Final Assessments. "Why not?" you ask. Because poor performers will weed themselves out before the Assessment, decreasing new hires by as much as 30% to 40%.

600,000 Pounds of Accountability

Using an analogy, if a truck carrying 40,000 pounds of meat from Canada into the United States fails the inspection, the next 15 trucks from that company will undergo the cost and inconvenience of an inspection, which equals inspecting 600,000 pounds of meat. In companies that hire a large number of salespeople annually, each hiring office will be audited for its training results by an outsider giving the Final Assessments. If the office's salespeople fail the Final Assessment, then the company will assess the next predetermined quantity of salespeople going through the office. The number of audits may range in the 50's, but will impact thousands.

Most on-line training programs include testing for knowledge, which is better than not testing at all. But what can't be tested for is the ability of a person to demonstrate his knowledge at a *"say and do"* level, under pressure to perform. It is this value that requires an assessor and differentiates the Accountability Performance System from any other training program or measurement system.

Surrounded By Technology

With the Accountability Performance System in place, you now have the ability to surround it with:

- Testing technology, and can meld the *Accelerated Learning Guide* into your selection process.

- Technology to monitor the progress for the learner as the learner completes the Checkpoints.

- Activity tracking technology that gives you feedback as to how well the learner is performing the business-generating activities necessary to be successful in the position.

- Video conferencing and teleconferencing that can be used to conduct Checkpoint Meetings and Final Assessments.

- Internet and intranet assignments which will reduce the amount of paper needed by the learner and will teach the learner to "fish" for information that is readily available if they would take the initiative to access it.

SURROUNDED BY TECHNOLOGY

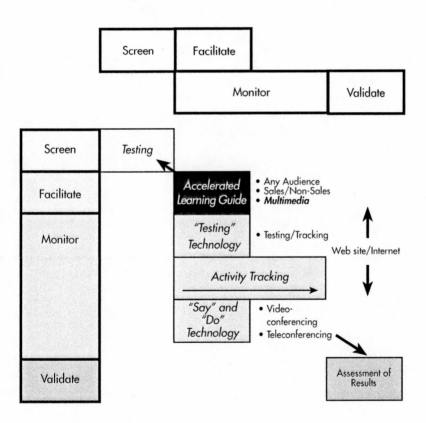

ACT FIVE: REVIEWS

Every theater fan, every actor, and every director is interested in the reviews. On opening night, it is traditional for the actors and the director to stay out for the evening until the first edition of the newspaper reveals the play's reviews.

Reviews

The following reviews come from companies who were clients of Frank Sarr. Pamela Truax conducted the interviews. Each client was asked if the Accountability Performance System fulfilled the system's five promises, plus four additional relevant questions. The questions were:

1. Did the Accountability Performance System accelerate the growth of your top performers? How?

2. Did the Accountability Performance System accelerate the identification of poor performers? How?

3. Did the Accountability Performance System get your own resources and the other training resources you wanted accessed used? How?

4. Did the system create top-down accountability for learning results and performance? How?

5. Did the system improve the effectiveness of the people—sales managers—who are implementing the training and have supervisory responsibilities? How?

6. Why was this approach to learning attractive to you when so many other training options and resources were available?

7. What kinds of problems did you feel that this approach addressed?

8. How long did it take from the beginning of the process until you felt like the process was in place and complete?

9. Did you do it first with existing staff, then with new hires—or how did that occur?

Review #1 from Charlotte

"I am blindly loyal to the Accountability Performance System; I've seen it work countless times. The first time I implemented the Accountability Performance System as a manager, we put healthy tension and accountability throughout our company and we made people prepare and perform. We made sales managers more accountable and salespeople more effective.

"The second time I implemented the Accountability Performance System, I brought Frank in to work with our bank-based insurance specialists and again accelerate the growth of 'keepers' and identify the poor performers. We had people actually resign rather than have to go through it—which was exactly what we were looking for, and so for me it proved the system is not industry-specific. If you use it the way it was designed, it will be consistent in its outcome."

1. **Did the process accelerate the growth of your top performers? How?**

    "Yes it did. For the same reason that the San Francisco 49ers go out and their first plays are all mapped and booked, our guys got the same confidence from this sales process. Secondly, the preparation is key; the 'keepers' took the time to rehearse and to plan for their performance. I think that is universal: musician, dancer, dentist, salesperson; you've got to sacrifice time from other things to prepare for your performance."

2. **Did the process accelerate the identification of poor performers? How?**

    "Yes. First, some were identified by self-acknowledgments; they would leave rather than go through the process. The poor performers could not answer the questions that others could answer with ease."

3. **Did the process leverage your own resources and the other training resources you wanted accessed? How?**

    "Two entities were held accountable, not just one. We've talked about the person to be trained, but it put equal responsibility on the trainers."

4. Did the process create top-down accountability for learning re-sults and performance? How?

"Salespeople, especially good ones, do not want structure, but they need it. Most of those I've seen in 26-27 years of management, tend to be product- rather than process-focused, and that's the beauty of this type of training program; it wraps a product around a process or a structure."

5. Did the system improve the effectiveness of the people—sales managers—who are implementing the training and have supervisory responsibilities? How?

"Yes, and just like it magnified poor sales performers, it magnified some poor management performers, too."

6. Why was this approach to learning attractive to you when so many other training options and resources were available to you?

"Are you asking, 'You have a floor and a half of training people, why wouldn't you go use them instead?' First, the training staff certainly does not have the years of experience that I can look to with the same confidence. Second, we don't have the kinds of tools inside ready to address the issues we have got. When we get to the Assessment, it tends to look homogeneous, like annual performance appraisals, rather than an initiative that is strategic and quantifiable... We always have the lack of time, resources, and budget internally to do it."

7. What kinds of problems were you attempting to address that you saw you could tackle with this approach?

"First, prospecting—taking a product and turning it into a process! Second, a structure that is well defined that can be used all the way from a brand new hire to your most seasoned veteran. It is learning versus training; they tend to forget the training, but the learning experience takes performance to a different level."

Review #2 from New York City (Health Care)

"We needed a simple way to get our story out, for sales people to sing off the same song sheet. A new hire is given a manual and told the Checkpoints. They self-study and review on a weekly or bi-weekly basis to make sure they are moving according to plan: 12 Checkpoints in 60 days. Then they sit down with me at the VP level and do a Final Assessment, graded and scored. Based on the grade, I can determine if they are passing or failing. This is a good barometer that they know what to take to the street, and through it they show a level of dedication. If not, we can weed them out with just cause.

"Changes in senior management were the original catalyst for applying the Accountability Performance System. Once people settled on a method, they wanted to take the temperature of the business so they assessed the entire group, from the VP level down and all got graded. It was pretty easy to pick out the stars from those who needed work."

1. Did the process accelerate the growth of your top performers? How?

"It tightened up their presentations."

2. Did the process accelerate the identification of poor performers? How?

"Absolutely. People whose numbers were solid, but were giving poor presentations were at risk of future losses. Through the Checkpoints and Final Assessments, we observed that their presentations were ineffective even though their numbers didn't show they had field challenges."

3. Did the process leverage your own resources and the other training resources you wanted accessed? How?

"Yes, it opened up a lot of dialog from other departments as well as sales. Because of the bits and pieces that people were charged with finding on their own, it created conversations within sales and identified lots of best practices."

4. **Did the process create top-down accountability for learning results and performance? How?**

"Yes. Since everything rolled up through the VP level, we became aware of what pieces of the puzzle were missing—like people having trouble defining managed care—so we added access to information for people, which tightened up many presentations. Also, since managers knew they were going in front of the VP's, they did not want their people reflecting poorly on them."

5. **Did the system improve the effectiveness of the people—sales managers—who are implementing the training and have supervisory responsibilities? How?**

"Absolutely. Prior to the Accountability Performance System, there was no format to learn the sales program. We say the assessment process gives them 'inch-deep, mile-wide information.' Then, as the need came up, they could go inch wide, mile deep."

6. **Why was this approach to learning attractive to you when so many other training options and resources were available to you?**

"We liked the idea of not having to have a full-time training person on site since we weren't hiring 6 or 8 or 10 people at a time, so having a full-time person did not make much sense. Also, the self-pacing made it more enjoyable for them and simultaneously showed us their ability to manage their own time and schedule. Managers could see how each person did learn and could feed them in their preferred way for their greatest effectiveness."

7. **What kinds of problems were you attempting to address that you saw you could tackle with this approach?**

"Lack of consistency in presentations; we specifically had the problem of people going out and presenting rates and network [managed care health care program] and presenting the same thing everyone in the industry was saying. We will win some and lose some that way, because of the competitive environment, so this taught them to talk about the big picture, where we come from, where we are going, the good news stories going on right now."

8. **What were your steps from the start to completion of the program... what did you set up in the way of meetings and Checkpoints to create this program and run it?**

"During the initial process, we said we were not going to scare anybody, but provide a learning experience that would benefit all employees. The sales force had trepidation that if they bombed the Assessment, they would be on the street. It created enough tension that people took it seriously. In contrast, before the Accountability Performance System, when handed information but not tested, salespeople glossed over the need to absorb the information. This time, when they knew senior-level managers were also taking the Assessment, they knew we were serious. Once through, we tabulated scores, figured out who did well and who bombed, tweaked the program, and then gave those who had done poorly a chance to represent themselves again. We posted the results showing who scored the highest and it was motivational. Some who did well wanted to do it again to get a higher score, which distinguished better talent and drive, versus the people who just wanted to do it and move on."

9. **How long did it take from the beginning of the process until you felt like the process was in place and complete?**

"Not long. Within 60 days, maybe 90 days on the outside."

10. **Did you do it first with existing staff, then with new people—or how did that occur?**

"We started with VP's, then managers, then the entire sales force went through the process and took the Assessment. Everybody saw that we implemented this process all the way to the top. We took this seriously."

Review #3 From Boston (Financial Services)

Background:

"We have a system of offices throughout the U.S. and our job was to set up a remote distance learning program for these 40 offices to educate and train the support staffs. Our accountability was to get them up to speed after a nationwide reorganization, so we were centralizing some accountabilities, localizing others. We were building a program to teach the new culture. Our task was less about top performers and more about very experienced, less experienced, and new people. The Accountability Performance System worked very well for this task. Our job was to find a common denominator and establish a baseline of knowledge. We did accomplish that."

1. Did the process accelerate the growth of your top performers? How?

"In one sense, yes—but it was designed to find a common denominator and create some kind of a culture among the 40 sales offices to be linked, and keep the communication lines open so people would not feel too detached. We were not trying to overcome anxiety, but some of that occurred as well."

2. Did the process leverage your own resources and the other training resources you wanted accessed? How?

"Yes, we had lots of resources and tools and materials with which to build a program. We combined existing resources with the organization and focus of the Accountability Performance System to create an effective program.

"When it was first applied, people were not used to the structure and accountability and people were a little 'testy' during the first two Checkpoints. But management hung in with us. They are still going today and not a whole lot differently than they were originally. We had a mission, we stuck to the plan, we were focused and we got there. After one year, we got more on autopilot so that the program could be self-administered."

3. Did the process accelerate the identification of poor performers? How?

"Yes, because of the newness of the program, they had structure, deadlines, readings, questionnaires, quizzes, and participation in conference calls, plus adjustments to their new jobs all at the same time. Some could handle it and some couldn't. The basic philosophy is that you are going to do as well on the training as on your job, so if you are sloppy in your learning exercises, you are probably that same person in your normal work. That weeded out some people all by itself."

4. **Did the process create top-down accountability for learning results and performance? How?**

"As you probably know, you can't get a program like this to persist without support of top management. We had support from top to bottom. There had to be buy-in from other supervisory areas and we got all that, so when we revealed underperformance, the supervisor needed to step in and make adjustments."

5. **Did the process improve the effectiveness of the managers who are implementing the training and supervisory responsibilities? How?**

"Yes, it was good for them because they learned more about the business. They did most of the work. It helped them to know what kind of person we need to do this job, giving them ability to assess whether the right candidates were coming to them and to assess these candidates' abilities."

6. **Why was this approach to learning attractive to you when so many other training options and resources were available to you?**

"The Accountability Performance System was more structured. Yet the structure was flexible enough that we would adapt for distance learning. We had the materials; it was a matter of putting in the right amounts and best subject matter so that people could digest the information without getting overwhelmed. We held Checkpoints via teleconferences to follow up and discuss, explain and demonstrate what they learned. Since they were communicating via telephone in their jobs, it was the perfect instrument for us to measure what they learned."

7. **What kinds of problems were you attempting to address that you saw this approach addressing?**

"The discipline, the accountability, the structure, the organization— we were able to use the Accountability Performance System as the template for our material."

8. How long did it take from your agreement to begin until you felt like the process was in place and complete?

"We are still doing it four years later! We still hold teleconferences, still disseminate batches of materials, still do homework, still conduct Assessments and Checkpoints. Quality is never out of style!"

9. Did you do it first with existing staff, then with new people—or how did that occur?

"We took them all through the process, maybe 65 or 70 people. Some had been here 20 years or more and some were brand new, some were transitioning from an old role into something new and we were trying to identify people we thought could do the new roles. So we had people who knew the company, but not the job. Fortunately, the ones who knew it were supportive and helpful and understood that we wanted to create common denominators. Meanwhile, the teleconferences became good sounding boards for people in transition to talk to each other."

10. What are those measurements?

"There's the turnover factor. For the most part, we have done a good job of hanging on to the people who have been trained. The people who have been here a long time stay, the middle group is stable, and the new group has the highest turnover.

"One measurement is that people have done a good job. We know by the job they do in the field, through feedback from coworkers, by how efficiently business is processed and goes through the system."

Review #4 from Wilkes-Barre (Health Care)

Background:

"We don't have a lot of representative turnover and we generally promote from within when we can. We are using it with new hires. Prior to this system, we tried to expose people to experience, gave them a book or brochure, but we did not give them the 'who, what, when, where, why' that the reps need to understand their jobs. The other nice thing is that as a manager, the Checkpoint approach benefits me because once per week I know I have these 15 minutes to do sales development, and then I can go off in other directions."

1. **Did the process accelerate the growth of your top performers? How?**

"Yes, it was tough because they didn't buy into it initially. But we had meetings every two weeks and as a group we devoted 45 minutes to Checkpoint Meetings. Whenever you put the existing sales group with a new person who is out-preparing a top performer, it puts pressure on the top performers to ramp up. Those not previously exposed to the organization did much better than the older employees at answering the questions."

2. **Did the process accelerate the identification of poor performers? How?**

"It did. It identified weaknesses, and the Checkpoints also identified stumbling blocks. Without a measurable approach, we had only our gut process; with the Checkpoints, it was great to be able to say, 'Go back, and redo that.'"

3. **Did the process leverage your own resources and the other training resources you wanted accessed? How?**

"Absolutely, particularly gaining effectiveness in the intranet and how to use the Internet."

4. **Did the process create top-down accountability for learning results and performance? How?**

"I would say bottom-up accountability! I understand what you mean, but it created accountability at the level of the people that went through the process. As a manager, I am a stakeholder and ultimately responsible for results, but the accountability really lies in each individual participant. For example, I went through the same process they did. However, if they did not do the assignments did it fall on my shoulders? No, the preparation went back on them."

5. **Did the process improve the effectiveness of the people—sales managers—who are implementing the training and supervisory responsibilities? How?**

"Oh yes. Because I had gone through it as well, they couldn't say, 'This is something the managers inflicted on me.' I could say, 'I recall in this section of the training manual it said this,' so it is almost embarrassing to challenge me on anything."

6. **Why was this approach to learning attractive to you when so many other training options and resources were available to you?**

"First is the accountability and second is that it is not classroom-based. I have people at different skill sets and education levels, so the fact that it points you to resources you can find and it teaches good habits are two additional things that I find attractive over other training options."

7. **What kinds of problems were you attempting to address that you saw this approach addressing?**

"Consistency was lacking prior to this. Originally, we wanted to see manuals, big binders. It was our expectation that when a training organization came, they would be armed with the traditional trappings. When we saw the more interactive, more self-directed approach, we were somewhat skeptical. After his analysis, Frank came back and said, 'You have got all this information, you already have a mission statement, what is the value of the salesperson understanding that mission statement?'"

8. **What were your steps from the start to completion of the program?**

"First we had sales training roll it out at a staff meeting to all our sales staff. Then we set up a Checkpoint three-month schedule at one time. We said, 'There is no reason that 60 days from now someone is going to spring a Checkpoint on you. You are in control.' Then we coordinated who would conduct Checkpoints and cross-regions, so I was getting out to other regional managers as well. Final evaluations were scheduled. We went through the set-up process in five days. In my area, I had 13 existing and two new employees for the initial program. At the end, we had a congratulatory event."

9. **How long did it take from your agreement to proceed until you felt like the process was in place and complete?**

"The process took two or three months to create and begin. Not long, really."

Additional Comments:

"There were some disappointments. Senior representatives looked at this as just an intrusion, saying, 'You are making me do this' rather than seeing it as an opportunity to improve ourselves. For some people, it was an opportunity to rise to the occasion and compete among their peers. They wanted to know to a tenth of a score how the person next to them did.

"There were some particularly pleasing surprises. One particular person who is in support, administrative operations, who could sit back and understand the sales process, got to be proactive in learning the salesperson's job. This was great because here was someone we knew at a basic level of competency who could say, 'Yes, I understand the salesperson's job.'"

Review #5 from Cleveland (Financial Services)

Background:

"At the time we were in an infancy business stage and employing new hires as quickly as possible. We realized we were not employing the right people, so we asked Frank to come in. The end product was a consolidation of a body of knowledge divided into eight Checkpoints."

1. **Did the process accelerate the growth of your top performers?**

"Not applicable because we were not differentiating top performers; we were working with new hires."

2. **Did the process accelerate the identification of poor performers?**

"Sure."

3. **Did the process leverage your own resources and the other training resources you wanted accessed?**

"Yes!"

4. **Did the process create top-down accountability for learning results and performance?**

"Yes."

5. **Did the process improve the effectiveness of the people—sales managers—who are implementing the training and supervisory responsibilities?**

"Yes."

6. **Why was this approach to learning attractive to you when so many other training options and resources were available to you?**

"This process was taking away our pain."

7. **What kinds of problems were you attempting to address that you saw this approach addressing?**

"We needed to integrate the agents into teams of bankers, and agents speak one language and bankers another. The agents learned how to speak 'bank-ese.' The agents learned the bankers' sales process; they knew how to integrate an insurance need into the bank sales process. They helped bankers identify a need and then to make the referral."

8. **What were your steps from the start to completion of the program?**

"This organization has many lines of business. The first Checkpoint dealt with the organization overall, its mission and values and how we are organized.

"The second Checkpoint dealt with our sales process. The Accountability Performance System created a sales process for an insurance specialist that was succinct and provided examples within the industry of why it works.

"After the sales process, the next Checkpoint was about financial planning and the tools and how to use them. Included were the fact finders that we use, and how to get acquainted with the type of technology that we use for the process of financial planning.

"The next Checkpoint dealt with how to work with internal centers of influence.

"Another Checkpoint was called product knowledge and processing new business.

"The next Checkpoint dealt with technology, and I mean at a very high level, the systems we use at our firm.

"Another Checkpoint dealt with a marketing plan. This plan asks them to identify what you are going to do to meet your goals and it provided an outline that they had to go through. It asked a series of questions and had them fill it out. Then it dealt with time and activities.

"The district manager was to coach the new hire through these resources in Checkpoint Meetings. The district manager would also use the *Accelerated Learning Guide* to review and confirm progress. These Checkpoints ensured that the new reps were communicating, at the same time the district manager was coaching for understanding. The new hires need to say, 'I can do it, I understand,' so during the Checkpoint Meeting, the rep was to demonstrate his understanding.

"At the end, there was comprehensive Final Assessment that actually assessed their knowledge that we used as a screening device."

ACCOUNTABILITY PERFORMANCE SYSTEM

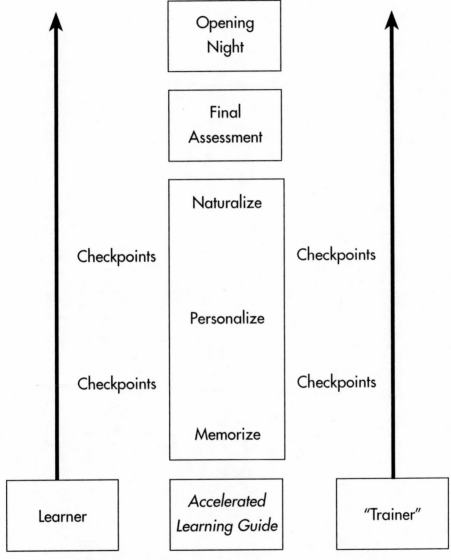

What are the roles of the learner, "trainer" and the
Accelerated Learning Guide to prepare for their opening night?

Conclusion

At the end of a successful performance, applause is warranted and welcomed. In this day and age, when your competitive advantage is the result of hiring and retaining the best people, you owe it to yourself and to your employees to address concerns about accountability and their future in a forthright and rational manner.

With this book, you have the framework to build your own Accountability Performance System, which will earn some deserved applause. If you need help to produce an *Accelerated Learning Guide* and implement the process, contact Training Implementation Services. Our web site is www.Performancecounts.com. Our telephone number is (860) 653-3575. Our e-mail address is info@Performancecounts.com.

APPENDIX

THE COMPANY
Sales Executives'/Client Managers'
Final Assessment

Name: _____

At this Assessment, you will be scored on your level of preparation for each competency. Your preparation will receive one of the following point values.

Outstanding	Above Average	Average	Below Average	Poor
4	3.5	3	2	1

Each competency has been given a specific amount of importance within the context of the overall Assessment. This importance is called Weight. The following scoring equation will be used to determine your total score for the Assessment: Preparation (x) Weight = Score.

---

1. The Company - (21 Points)

Preparation (x) Weight = Score

(Must be able to...)

A. Describe <u>The Company's</u> philosophy
    and history.   ____(0.75)____

B. Discuss <u>The Company's</u> mission, vision and operating
    principles.   ____(0.75)____

C. Discuss the roles and responsibilities of the subsidiaries,
    affiliates, and/or major business units that make up
    <u>The Company.</u>   ____(0.75)____

D. Discuss and identify <u>The Company's</u> key players, key
    issues and strategies.   ____(1.00)____

E. Explain what makes <u>The Company</u> different from its
    competitors.   ____(1.00)____

F. Demonstrate how you would tell someone about
    <u>The Company.</u>   ____(1.00)____

Comments:

Final Assessment
(continued)

2. The Franchise - (30 Points)

Preparation (x) **Weight** = **Score**

(Must be able to...)

A. Explain what is meant by "The Franchise."   ___(1.00)___

B. Explain the characteristics required to be a successful
    franchisee.   ___(1.00)___

C. Explain how **you** are compensated.   ___(0.75)___

D. Discuss the role agents and brokers play in the success
    of your franchise.   ___(1.00)___

E. Demonstrate how you would explain to a producer our
    compensation and incentive programs.   ___(0.75)___

F. Describe the importance of account management to the
    success of your franchise.   ___(0.75)___

G. Describe the critical components of account management.   ___(0.75)___

H. Describe the types of strategies that you use to impact the
    success of your franchise in your territory.   ___(0.75)___

I. Discuss your definition of a "client" and what is required
    to turn a customer into a client.   ___(0.75)___

Comments:

Final Assessment
(continued)

Assessment Summary

	Potential Points	Actual Points
1. The Company	21	_____
2. The Franchise	30	_____
3. The Financials	24	_____
4. Value-Based Selling	25	_____

Total Score   (100)   _____

Administered by: _____ **Date :** _____

The above assessment summary reflects the technical knowledge of the participant. The following table will reflect the "style" score. A score of (1) indicates the material was memorized and recited in a rote style. On the other hand, a score of (6) indicates the knowledge was explained and discussed in a naturalized manner that demonstrated mastery of the material.

Presentation Score
(a ✔ will indicate the level of naturalization demonstrated by the participant)

Memorized		Personalized		Naturalized	
1	2	3	4	5	6

Understanding ⟶ Ability To Communicate

Comments:

THE COMPANY
Sales Executives'/Client Managers'
Results/Action Steps

Name: _____

Office: _____

Director: _____

Vice President: _____

Assessment Score: (_____)

100-85	Congratulations! It is obvious that you have worked hard to achieve this level of competency.
84-75	You still need work in a few areas, but good effort.
74 and Below	Unsatisfactory. You need more work. We must identify the next steps to take to get you on target with the rest of your associates.

Recommended Next Steps

- Areas which need improvement are:

_____

_____

_____

_____

- Redo the following areas of the *Accelerated Learning Guide* and take the Assessment over again on _____ *(record the date).*

_____

_____

_____

_____

Signed by: _____ Date: _____

THE COMPANY'S

Accelerated Learning Guide

Table of Contents
Accelerated Learning Guide

Implementation Overview

Self-Directed

A self-directed approach to learning means that you will be responsible for completing the learning activities as defined in a Checkpoint Unit.

Your director will:
- Monitor the completion of each of the Checkpoint Units.
- Serve as a facilitator of your learning by having you demonstrate that you can communicate to him/her what you have learned.

The Three Components

The three components of our approach to learning are:
1. The Final Assessment.
2. The *Accelerated Learning Guide*.
3. The Internet/intranet (existing resources).

1. The Final Assessment

The Final Assessment is the focal point of your learning experience. The Final Assessment is where you will be expected to demonstrate proficiency after you have completed the assignments and activities in the *Guide*.

The idea behind this learning experience is "to begin with the end in mind." Therefore, we suggest you review the Final Assessment before starting the Checkpoints. This review will give you a sound basis for the learning that needs to occur.

The Final Assessment can be found in your *Guide* at the tab marked "Final Assessment." At the Final Assessment:
- You will discuss, explain and demonstrate your knowledge of the material listed in the Final Assessment at a one-on-one session with an assessor, and
- Your answers will be evaluated and scored by your assessor. (An explanation of the scoring methodology can be found in the Appendix tab.)

If, after reviewing and testing your ability to communicate the material being assessed, you feel you are prepared to perform and score well when taking your Final Assessment, then there is no need to delve into the *Accelerated Learning Guide*.

Implementation Overview
(continued)

2. *Accelerated Learning Guide*

The *Accelerated Learning Guide* contains Checkpoints which are subject matter-specific and are designed to accelerate your learning and preparation for the Final Assessment by:

- Directing you to those resources that will specifically provide the information that you need in order to learn what is expected. This helps eliminate the time and energy wasted hunting for answers.
- Identifying what to look for and where to find the answers within sometimes voluminous content.
- Sending you through a series of steps that increase your ability to retain and apply what you have learned.

The *Accelerated Learning Guide* also:

- Serves as a "road map" for the resources you'll need to complete each assignment, and
- Provides a structured process for the learning that has to take place.

Proper use of the *Accelerated Learning Guide* can result in learning and retention that is far superior to the traditional classroom and/or learn by the "seat of your pants" method.

3. Internet/Intranet (Existing Resources)

You will be directed as much as possible to the Internet and/or company intranet to obtain the information required to prepare for your Checkpoint Meetings and Final Assessment. This is done because we want you to:

- Have access to the most current information, and
- Use these resources because that will make you more effective in your performance of your responsibilities.

Expectations

You will be expected to:

- Complete all the assignments and activities in this *Accelerated Learning Guide.*
- Attend the Checkpoint Meetings and be prepared to demonstrate your ability to apply the assigned material.
- Pass the Final Assessment.

Learning Process

STEP ONE	*Understand the flow of each Checkpoint that is included in the* Accelerated Learning Guide.

Accelerated Learning Guide

The *Accelerated Learning Guide* is a "road map" that directs you to the appropriate resources that will enable you to develop the desired competencies. To facilitate the learning process, Checkpoints have been established where you focus in on a subject matter area that is critical to your success. Each Checkpoint is organized in the following manner:

1. *Content*

The content sets the stage for each Checkpoint. We want you to understand why the Checkpoint topic is important and outline the resources that are necessary to complete the Checkpoint.

2. *Checkpoint Assignments*

The Checkpoint Assignments will direct you to review, read, and access resources to complete each assignment.

3. *Application Questions*

Next to each assignment are Application Questions. These are the questions that you will be expected to answer orally in a clear, prepared manner at the Checkpoint Meeting with your facilitator.

4. *Learning Activities*

After the Checkpoint Assignments and questions, there are Learning Activities that you need to complete.

Learning Process
(continued)

STEP TWO	*Utilize the resources assigned to complete the assignment.*

The Company's Resources

The intent of the road map is to make certain that we not only get you to all the appropriate resources, but just as importantly, that you utilize these valuable resources at the correct point in your development.

Resources can include content contained in the *Accelerated Learning Guide*, the Internet, <u>The Company's</u> intranet, manuals, people, multimedia, brochures, scripts, video tapes, worksheets/forms, etc.

STEP THREE	*Prepare for and participate in a Checkpoint Meeting.*

"I Do. I Understand."

Our approach to your training and development is based upon asking you to **do** so you will **understand**—thus, "I Do. I Understand."

Whether you meet with a director, learning facilitator, another person, or no one at all, the expectation is that you will be able to answer orally the Application Questions for all the assignments made in the Checkpoint. You may be asked all or selected questions for each assignment in the Checkpoint. When asked the questions, your answers will be assessed on the level of **preparation** evidenced by your oral answers. (See *Performance Evaluation* in the Appendix tab.)

Learning Process
(continued)

Using Your Communication Skills

Each Checkpoint Meeting is an opportunity to demonstrate the qualities needed to be successful in any position—initiative, preparation and the ability to control your own destiny. In many respects, it is a role-play in which you are demonstrating your communication skills using critical knowledge as the basis of the role-play.

STEP FOUR	*Participate in a Final Assessment.*

"Begin with the end in Mind."

The Final Assessment encompasses all the areas in which you must be proficient in order to move successfully to the next step of the development process. This is the ultimate role-play in which you demonstrate your ability to perform your role as defined for this point in your development. As you mature in your role and development process, the expectations and the level of proficiency change.

Learning Process
(continued)

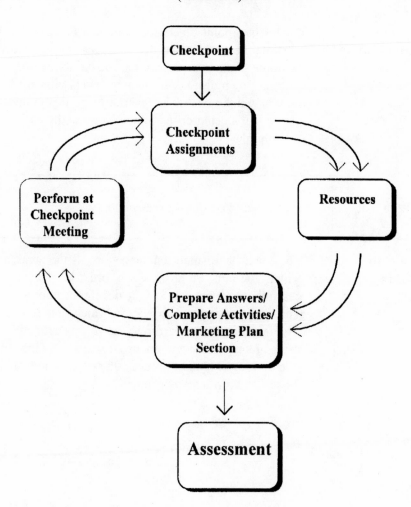

**Learning Process = Trainee Does 80% of the Preparation/
Trainee Retains 60–80% of the knowledge**

**Training Process = Trainer Does 80% of the Preparation/
Trainee Retains 10–30% of the knowledge**

"I Do. I Understand."

Our Approach

A Stanford University study established that when a person hears an idea once, he/she forgets 68% of it in 48 hours and more than 90% of it in 30 days. Supporting this claim is the saying:

"I hear, I forget.
I see, I may remember.
I do. I understand."
Confucius (451 BC)

Retaining What You Have Learned

Our approach to your training and development is based upon asking you to **do** so you will **understand**, thus "I Do. I Understand."

First, we feel that if an idea is important enough for us to include in this *Accelerated Learning Guide*, then it is equally important for you to retain more than 10% of the idea at the end of 30 days. Second, in order to increase the retention, we have to implement *a process* that will encourage and support greater retention—that is why the emphasis is on, "I Do. I Understand."

"I Do. I Understand."

"I Do. I Understand." This means to us that someone has taken the resources they have been provided and has completed the work necessary to say and do something that demonstrates that they have learned what they need to learn. To get to this point, the trainee will have to read, hear and/or see something.

Continuum of Retention

90% Do
70% Say
40% Hear and See
20% Hear
10% Read

Performance Counts

Have You Read the Material? Yes.

There is generally an enthusiastic response when this question is asked of an individual or a group. *"Yes, we have."* In most cases, the assignment was read. The number of pages may have been more than was expected but it was read-even though interest in the reading waned close to the end of the reading assignment and there were a couple of interruptions while completing the assignment.

Do You Understand What You Have Read? Yes.

"The reading material wasn't all that complicated, so there wasn't too much that had to be done to understand the material."

"If It Is Not Clear in Your Mind, It Will Sound Worse When You Speak It."

There is no question that the person read the assignment. There is no question that the person understood the content to a certain level-the fill-in-the-blank or multiple-choice level. But did the person understand this material at the level required to communicate their understanding in a clear, prepared manner? In other words, did the person really understand what he/she read?

A Different Expectation/ a Different Level of Tension

What happens when you are expected to move from the "fill-in- the-blank/multiple choice level" to the communication level?
1. We now know whether you understand or do not understand what you have read.
2. In order to communicate what you have read or the understanding of an activity that you have performed, you have to:
   - Read the material; complete the activity.
   - Internalize the material and/or activity so that you are truly putting forth the effort required to understand what was assigned.
   - Practice presenting the content until it is not only correct, but also demonstrates a level of understanding that allows you to communicate it in a manner that is understandable to the person to whom you are speaking.

Learning Process

(continued)

The Fifteen-Minute Reading Assignment/ Activity

The fifteen minutes of reading that is required to prepare us to perform at the first level-the fill-in-the-blank/multiple choice level-could turn into a one- or-two-hour effort. This all depends on the individual who is attempting to come prepared to communicate their understanding of what they have read, viewed or done and the subject matter. What changes have to occur when you move from one level to the next?

Sense Of Urgency/ Motivation

I am going to have to perform. I do not want to embarrass myself.

Retention

It is now clear in my mind. I now under-stand what this is all about.

Tension Level

I'd better come prepared. I am going to have to perform.

Performance Counts

The retention, the ability to apply what you have learned, the personal satisfaction that comes from intense preparation, and the differentiation of you from your peers and competitors is what makes performance count. Failure to make the effort up front to do what is required to thoroughly prepare yourself to perform at your best at all times will impact your success in any capacity.

Checkpoint Flow

Checkpoint Flow	This is the flow of the content found in this *Accelerated Learning Guide*, and the areas that you must be competent in to perform your responsibilities.
The Company	It is important that you not only know whom you are working for but also where the organization wants to go. Because if the organization is going to get there, you are going to have to help!
	This step covers The Company's vision, mission, who we are and the preparation it takes to tell someone about The Company in a prepared, professional manner. This is what helps deliver the critical first impression with a prospect, broker and/or client.
The Franchise	This is the mind-set that The Company wants their Sales Executives/Client Managers to have about the way they will operate their business. In many respects, you operate as the owner of a franchise. How does this ownership impact the way that you perform your daily business activities?
	As an owner of a franchise, you have to operate with an intensity and focus that is different than if you viewed yourself as an employee. Besides having the attitude of a franchise owner, you must also be prepared to perform all the daily activities and implement the processes required to make your franchise successful.

Checkpoint Flow
(Continued)

The Financials

In order for your franchise to be successful, it must be profitable. If a franchise is not profitable, it shows up in the owner's pocket. Do you understand what it takes to make your "franchise" profitable?

Every piece of business that you submit and renew carries with it a level of profitability. You have to know what that level is so that you can determine how hard you want to fight to have a piece of business delivered and supported by The Company. As a salesperson, you want every piece of business serviced by The Company. As a franchise owner, would you use the same criteria to judge a piece of business?

Value-Based Selling

Not only does a franchise have standards and processes for manufacturing their products in their remote locations, but they also have standards and processes that establish how their people will interact with their customers.

The Company has established Value-Based Selling as the standard used when interacting with their customers. Inherent in Value-Based Selling is the process that a person must follow to perform in a manner that differentiates The Company salesperson from their competition because of their commitment to and their ability to deliver Value-Based Selling.

Checkpoint Meeting
Performance Evaluation Form

Name:_____ Date: _____
Checkpoint: _____ Facilitator: _____

Directions: Upon completion of each Checkpoint, evaluate the performance of each participant based on the "Indicators of Preparation" shown below.

"If a thought is not clear in our minds, it will not be clear when we speak it."

Indicators of Preparation

Use of the Pause	Answers	Participation	Eye Contact	Spontaneity
Instead of "um.," "you know," "aah, ok?", the presenter uses silence to prepare to answer.	Presents concise, thought-out answers with a minimum of rambling or unnecessary elaboration or clarification.	Is ready when called upon to answer the question and is proactive in sharing constructive thoughts with the other participants.	Maintains eye contact and looks at you when giving the answer.	Responds to additional clarifying questions you may ask.

Evaluation of Performance

High (H)	Average (A)	Poor (P)
Meets and exceeds the specific indicators of preparation.	In these specific areas of preparation she has not distinguished herself from the other participants.	Not prepared in these specific areas.

1. ASSIGNMENTS/ANSWERS

Directions: *Next to the appropriate assignment, circle your evaluation of the participant's performance.*

Assignment #	Subject Matter (Optional)	Evaluation
Assignment 1		High/Average/Poor
Assignment 2		High/Average/Poor
Assignment 3		High/Average/Poor
Assignment 4		High/Average/Poor
Assignment 5		High/Average/Poor
Assignment 6		High/Average/Poor

Based on the trainee's responses, what is your overall assessment of his/her preparation? Prepared: _____   Unprepared: _____

2. ACTIVITIES

Were the activities required for this Checkpoint completed satisfactorily? Please Explain Below.

_____

_____

3. OBSERVATIONS

Complete the following categories by writing down your overall thoughts and any problems you perceive about this trainee's performance.

COMMUNICATION (Knowledge/Skills) - (e.g., needs help understanding the material) _____

_____

_____

ATTITUDE - (e.g., approaching assignments with a poor attitude)

_____

_____

HABIT - (e.g., once again has not completed all the assignments)

_____

_____

4. DIAGNOSIS

		Yes	No
A.	Is there a performance discrepancy?	_____	_____
B.	Is it a knowledge/skill deficiency?	_____	_____
C.	Is it an attitude/habit deficiency?	_____	_____
D.	Does he/she have what it takes?	_____	_____

5. NEXT STEPS

ACTIVITIES:

_____

_____

OBJECTIVES:

_____

_____

Date of Next Checkpoint Meeting: _____   Checkpoint # _____

Checkpoint One
What Do You Know About <u>The Company</u>?

Learning Context

One of the strengths of top performers is that they believe in their company and products. It shows in the enthusiasm they project when talking about either. Top performers are motivated by the strengths of their organization and the excellence of their products and services. Armed with knowledge, passion and skill, top performers are able to emphasize and highlight the advantages of their organization.

Obviously, there are always stresses and strains in daily business life. However, despite the problems and concerns of daily activities, top performers are sustained by a belief in their company and the products and services they offer.

Objective

Top performers are still able to present the positives about their company and products in a very clear and enthusiastic manner. They know that they ARE the company, and sooner or later the prospect/client is going to want to know that the company itself is the right choice for them. So, the objective of this Checkpoint is to:

- Help you understand why you need to know as much about The Company as possible.
- Show you where you can go to get the information you need and instruct you to go to these sources to begin to integrate this knowledge into your sales process.
- Prepare you to use this knowledge so that it does not interfere with your primary objective, which is to find out as much as you can about the prospect and/or client so that you can make a sale, retain the business, or expand and sell additional products and services to the account.

Important Data

The Company data is information that can or will be a part of the decision-making process of the buyer. It should be fine-tuned so that it is part of your sales process and your relationship-building repertoire.

"What Do You Know About The Company?"

To perform your task successfully, you need to spend the time and effort preparing yourself to be able to answer the question "What Do You Know About The Company?" In probably all instances, the person to whom you are speaking does not know all he/she needs to know to understand the benefits of a relationship with The Company. He/she may even have a poor impression of The Company. It is your responsibility to educate them about The Company and the benefits of finding out more about what you can do for them. The remaining content will help prepare you to perform this critical responsibility.

Company Knowledge: The Basis of Trust

If you were asked by someone to tell them about The Company:
- What would you tell them?
- How would you tell them about your company?
- When do you tell them about your company?

Whether you are asked or whether you tell a prospect or client about your company, it is important that you know everything you can about it for the following reasons:

1. You never know what a prospect or client is going to ask you.
2. Whether they ask or not, thorough company knowledge is the basis of a trusting relationship. Whenever possible, a prospect/client should receive information about your company directly from you and not from an outside source. Depending on the nature of their sources, they may hear something that you may not want them to hear.

3. The more you know about <u>The Company</u>, the more likely it is that you will use information about <u>The Company</u> to gain credibility in the eyes of your prospect/client.

4. The more you know, the more enthusiastic you will be when telling the prospect/client about <u>The Company</u>. Enthusiasm is an important element in demonstrating why you are different in the eyes of the prospect/client.

What Do You Tell the Prospect or Client?

The more you know about something, the better the chances of selecting the appropriate information to share with someone. What information should you have in your portfolio to tell the prospect about <u>The Company</u>?

You could tell them about its:

• Vision
• Mission
• Values
• Markets/Marketing Strategy
• Size
• Growth
• Unique advantages

There may be other items that you may want to share, but whatever the information, know what it is and have it available to share when needed.

The Focal Point Is <u>The Company</u>!

In the long term, your prospect/client is buying the products and services of <u>The Company</u>. You work hard at building a trusting relationship with your prospect/client but, ultimately, <u>The Company</u> is their focal point. The primary reason that you want to tell the prospect/client about <u>The Company</u> is to enable them to obtain some understanding of the company with which they will be ultimately working.

(Checkpoint Content Continues Until Assignment Portion of Checkpoint)

Checkpoint One
What Do You Know About <u>The Company</u>?
(continued)

Date To Be Completed: _____
Complete the questions following each assignment.

Assignment 1—Read: "What Do You Know About <u>The Company</u>?", Checkpoint One Introduction

1. Why is it important that you know everything you can about your company?
2. Define "Winging-it." How can you prevent this from happening during a meeting?
3. Where in the meeting do you introduce your company? Why?
4. What are your objectives for doing research about your company?
5. What are some of the research sources available to you?
6. Who is <u>The Company</u>?
7. What is <u>The Company</u>:
    • Vision?
    • Mission?
8. What are our values and our principles of integrity?
9. Why is it important to understand the financial strength of your company?
10. How can the Best's Ratings and the Standard & Poor's Ratings help you understand the financial strength of <u>The Company</u>?

Assignment 2—Review: Annual Report, *Our Formula for Success*

1. What is the theme of the Annual Report?
2. Explain how this was a successful year for both <u>The Company</u> and for the public we serve.
3. Explain <u>The Company</u> At-A-Glance.
4. Explain the following business strategies that are transforming <u>The Company</u> into a savvier consumer-focused organization:
    • Consumer Health Management   • Quality Improvement
    • Product Innovation   • Customer Service
    • Marketing Successes   • Government Business
    • Financial Performance
5. What are some examples of <u>The Company</u>'s meaningful Health Care Partnerships?
6. Explain how <u>The Company</u> is an integral and influential part of the community itself.
7. Explain our financial position and operating results.

Checkpoint One
What Do You Know About <u>The Company</u>?
(continued)

Assignment 3—Read: The Business of <u>The Company</u>
1. Who is <u>The Company</u>?
2. Who do we serve?
3. What are <u>The Company</u>'s traditional products?
4. What are <u>The Company</u>'s managed care products?
5. What are <u>The Company</u>'s Supplemental products?

Assignment 4—Access: <u>The Company</u> Web site
www.thecompany.com
1. What information can be found about <u>The Company</u>?
2. In general, what do the following categories tell you about <u>The Company</u>:
    • News and Info
    • About <u>The Company</u>
    • Employment
    • Medicare
    • Health
    • Dental
    • Vision
    • Life and Casualty
3. How can this site help you to keep current and to prepare your company introduction paragraph?

Assignment 5—Access: <u>The Company</u> Web site
www.thecompany.com
1. In your opinion, why is it important for every <u>Company</u> employee to access this *Code of Business Conduct* site?
2. The Code is made up of specific policies we each must follow, as our jobs dictate. The Code's policies are organized into what nine Guideposts?
3. Explain how this Code is part of our broader Integrity Process.
4. Our Code of Business Conduct reflects the company's commitment to what?
5. If you suspect a violation of the Corporate Code of Business Conduct, to whom should you report your concerns?

Learning Activities

Activity 1:   Put yourself in the prospect's/client's shoes and build a
                     list of questions they might ask about <u>The Company</u>.

Activity 2:   Have a drilled and rehearsed company introduction to be
                     used as part of an individual or group presentation.

Activity 3:   Complete <u>The Company</u> Section (1) of your Marketing
                     Plan. **(Appendix Tab)**

What Do You Know About
<u>The Company?</u>

ACTIVITY 1

Activity	*Objectives*
Please Answer for Me . . . 	• To put yourself in the prospect's/client's shoes and build a list of questions they might ask. • To develop the answers to respond to these questions.
Resources 	A) Annual Report B) Marketing Literature C) Other marketing resources D) Other people in the company or outside the company E) Any other resources that, through your independent efforts, you determine can help you with this activity
Instructions 	1. You are not an employee of the company but a prospect or client being approached by a salesperson from the company. Based on the research you have just completed, list 10 questions that you as the prospect/client would possibly ask about the company. 2. Once you have developed your ten (10) questions, write the answers to the questions on the following worksheet. 3. Be prepared to role-play your introduction with your learning facilitator.

What Do You Know About <u>The Company</u>? (1)

Please answer for me . . .

Questions	Answers
1.	
2.	
3.	
4.	
5.	

What Do You Know About The Company? (1)

Please answer for me . . .

Questions	Answers
6.	
7.	
8.	
9.	
10.	

Frank W. Sarr, MAT
Orchestrating Extraordinary Training Performances

Frank Sarr is Owner/President of Training Implementation Services, a company founded in 1990 on the premise that the real genius is not in building training programs, but in getting them used. His approach to implementation has produced extraordinary training performances in the life insurance, banking and managed care industries for his client companies.

Mr. Sarr had an 18-year association with Connecticut General/CIGNA, where he served as vice president of all field training, including management development. He also worked for the Wilson Learning Corporation. There he marketed training products to the financial services industry throughout the United States, Australia and Canada.

Mr. Sarr received a Bachelor of Arts degree in Economics from the University of Notre Dame and a Master of Arts degree in Teaching from Oberlin College.

Pamela Larson Truax, MBA, CPCM
Bridging the gap between people and profitability

Pamela Larson Truax is the President of Accountability Pays, a company that is on a crusade to exponentially and measurably improve the way people are hired and developed. Being accountable is a bottom line phenomenon that happens through employees (who are always people). Accountability Pays provides direct and indirect corporate support to help companies select and develop people—the human capital that generates profitability.

Two issues impact a person's ability to do their job effectively. One is eligibility (*can* the person do the job; that is, can she acquire or does she have mastery of the required competencies) and the other is suitability (*will* the person do the job). The Accountability Performance System addresses eligibility and the Harrison InnerView addresses suitability.

In addition to providing corporate consulting, Accountability Pays is a licensing agency for the Accountability Performance System and the Harrison InnerView. The Accountability Performance System is the subject of this book. The Harrison InnerView is the only assessment tool on the market that predicts job success. It identifies specific traits that are essential for success in a particular job and also isolates specific traits that are predictors of failure of that job. Used to its fullest potential, the Harrison InnerView is a Performance Management System.

Pamela has been marketing director for the Ken Blanchard Companies International Division, and has trained and spoken around the world. Past clients include Kodak and SKF. She is a Certified Professional Consultant to Management (CPCM), author, facilitator, and consultant. Pamela has an MBA from the University of San Diego.

You can reach Pamela Truax at 858-486-8606 or 888-2 GUIDE U, or via e-mail at Truax@accountabilitypays.com. The web site is www.accountabilitypays.com.

Tony Alessandra, Ph.D.
Building Customers, Relationships, and the Bottom Line

Dr. Tony Alessandra, author of the business bestsellers *Non-Manipulative Selling* and *The Art of Managing People*, helps companies achieve market dominance through specific strategies designed to outmarket, outsell, and outservice the competition. Audiences learn how to get and keep profitable customers by applying Dr. Alessandra's high-tech and high-touch marketing, sales, service, and relationship-building skills.

Dr. Alessandra has a street-wise, college-smart perspective on business, having fought his way out of Hell's Kitchen in NYC to eventually realizing success as a graduate professor of marketing, business author, and co-founder of MentorU.com, an on-line e-learning company of world-class business experts providing training and coaching utilizing the latest Internet technologies.

Dr. Alessandra earned his MBA from the University of Connecticut—and his Ph.D. in marketing from Georgia State University. Recognized by *Meetings & Conventions* magazine as "one of America's most electrifying speakers," he was inducted into the Speakers Hall of Fame in 1985—and is a member of the Speakers Roundtable, a group of 20 of the world's top professional speakers.

Dr. Alessandra is a widely published author with 13 books translated into 11 foreign languages, including *Charisma* (Warner Books, 1998); *The Platinum Rule* (Warner Books, 1996); *Collaborative Selling* (John Wiley & Sons, 1993); and *Communicating at Work* (Fireside/Simon & Schuster, 1993). He's been featured in 50 audio/video programs, including **Relationship Strategies**, **The Dynamics of Effective Listening,** and **The 10 Qualities of Charismatic People** (all Nightingale Conant); *Relationship Strategies* (American Media); and **Non-Manipulative Selling** (Walt Disney).

Tony Alessandra reaches people—from the Board of Directors to the front-line folks in the trenches. He gets across information "with a lot of snap"—so people can grasp it, remember it, and use it.

You can reach Dr. Alessandra at www.alessandra.com or Tony@Alessandra.com or (800) 459-4515

Footnotes

i.   Smart, Bradford D., Ph.D., <u>Top Grading</u>, Prentice Hall, 1999, page 46.
ii. Louis Harris and Associates, 1999.
iii. "Love the Battle," Pathways To Performing Your Best Under Competitive Pressure, James E. Loehr, Ed.D.

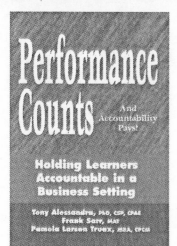

Share it with others!

To order individual copies of this book:

Phone: (860) 653-3575

Fax: (860) 653-9238

Mail: 522B Salmon Brook Street, Granby, CT 06035

Payable in U. S. funds only. Book price: $25.00 each copy, $30.00 Canadian. Postage and handling U.S./Canada is $2.75 for one book, $1.00 for each additional book. Please add 6% sales tax for all orders within Connecticut. We will accept your check for the full amount. ($15.00 fee for each returned check). Sorry, no cash or COD orders.

Special bulk discounts are available.

Please send _____ copies of *Performance Counts*.

Total for books $ _____

Applicable sales tax $ _____

Postage & handling $ _____

Total Amount due $ _____

☐ I am enclosing a check for $_____.

☐ Please bill my credit card   __Visa   ___MC   Card No. _____

Expiration Date: _____   Signature _____

Name _____

Company _____

Address _____

_____

City, State, Zip _____

Daytime phone _____

Ship to (if different):

Name _____

Company _____

Address _____

_____

City, State, Zip _____

Please allow 4–6 weeks weeks delivery.